W9-APH-320

The

Bliss Principle

5 EASY WAYS TO REDUCE STRESS

cds
BOOKS

Copyright © 2005 Kellye Davis

All rights reserved. No part of this book may be reproduced or transmitted in any form or by any means, electronic or mechanical, including photocopying and recording, or by any information storage or retrieval system, without written permission from Kellye Davis, CDS Books, or the respective copyright holders.

For information please address:

CDS Books
425 Madison Avenue
New York, NY 10017

ISBN: 1-59315-203-5

Orders, inquiries, and correspondence should be addressed to:

CDS Books
425 Madison Avenue
New York, NY 10017
(212) 223-2969 FAX (212) 223-1504

Printed in the United States of America

10   9   8   7   6   5   4   3   2   1

This book is dedicated to
Vernez Kittrell
(June 23, 1959–June 1, 2002)

my sister,
confidante, and friend.

May we meet—again and again and again.

Acknowledgments

I wish to acknowledge all the people, places, and things that supported me in writing this book. I wish to thank my entire family. My mother, who showed me the power of trusting my instincts; my father, for his loving ways; André, for keeping the love flowing; Rudy, for his positive words; my girlfriends, for putting up with me not returning calls right away; Ms. Brown, for her positive feedback. I wish to acknowledge all the typists who helped mc typc and typc and type some more—as well as my office staff, including Amanda Kraemer, for being there every day. I would also like to acknowledge the beautiful beach in Pompano Beach, Florida, for being there for me when I needed to be inspired as well as my creative colleagues: Ann Gayler for her illustrations, and Marcia Clarke for her creative coaching. I wish to thank the editorial team at CDS Books and David Wilk. I'd also like to thank Dennis Swanson and Robert Branch for giving me an opportunity in television. I'd like to acknowledge those spiritual leaders who've inspired me throughout the years: Deepak Chopra and the host of yoga masters of modern and ancient times for leading a pathway to follow. I wish to thank my students and clients who've trusted me throughout the years and to acknowledge Swami Chidvilasananda for her unfathomable guidance.

Table of Contents

The
Bliss Principle

A Quest for Peace

As long as you live, keep learning how to live.

—SENECA

*H*ow often have you felt the urge to submerge yourself in a few moments of peace and tranquility during your day? Maybe you're stalled in a long line at Starbucks, chained to your desk, or trying to break up a squabble among your kids—again. If only you could take a mental time-out to momentarily get away from it all . . . work just part-time . . . quit your job once and for all . . . hire someone to be you . . . go on that much-needed vacation.

If only. Without question, we live in stressful times, an era in which we're expected to do more, be more things to more people, never say no. Of course, you juggle the responsibilities, obligations, and constant change the best way you can. Yet it's safe to say that many of us are tired, stressed out, beaten down, and psychologically fragile from giving our all every day. We long for escape. Still, we're stuck—in traffic, on deadline, with the overwhelming to-do list that is our lives. Many of us are subtly suffering for it, whether it is in the form of chronic tension, a raging headache, difficulty concentrating, heart palpitations, insomnia, a short temper, a generalized feeling of anxiety, or perhaps even more overt, diagnosable conditions, such as panic disorder, irritable bowel syndrome, or digestive problems.

As a restorative yoga teacher and level II Reiki healer in the New York City metropolitan area for over a decade, I see the frazzled minds and tired bodies of those I teach every day. There's Jack, for example, a father of four who experienced a series of traumatic events. His wife had died of cancer and he lost many friends in the attack on the World Trade Center on September 11. He was so filled with anxiety and despair that he was taking antidepressants to cope with his pain. His sagging posture suggested hopelessness. "I'm overwhelmed by my life," he said.

Doris, a political campaign manager, also comes to mind. Consumed with her professional responsibilities, she found it a torment to simply relax and lie still in the various yoga poses I suggested during our sessions. "I keep thinking, 'What will the newspaper headlines say about my candidate? What dress should I wear to tomorrow night's fundraiser?' It's all I can do not to run out of the room to check my voice mail," she confessed one day. Doris had an extreme case of what's known as the "monkey mind," a racing mind that won't quit.

Doris has plenty of company. Many of my clients relay that on more days than not, they sprint through life, fueled by adrenaline. "Yesterday, I was so busy, I didn't eat breakfast until dinnertime," said Sophie, a single mother of three, only half joking.

In the midst of their multitasking schedules, they may be irritable or impatient with their partner or their children. Exhausted by it all, they may find themselves unable to sleep, unable to concentrate, unable even to take a breather and just relax. "It's hard for me to sit through a movie," said Renee, a twenty-seven-year-old unemployed insurance executive who was job hunting. Some of my clients tell me they're taking Provigil, a prescription drug purported to promote alertness better than caffeine. But they come to my classes looking like they need a good night's sleep. "Help!" one pleaded.

I've certainly had my own share of stress. In fact, the desire to find inner peace and move beyond the worldly drains of daily life was what drew me to meditation and yoga in the first place. As my meditation skills developed, I was freed up to enter and access the center of peace inside my soul. And thanks to the guidance of my meditation teacher, I was shown that I was much more than the stress in my life. What I learned became the impetus for my Bliss Life Program on a very personal level.

As a wellness journalist, stress management counselor, certified yoga instructor, and ongoing student of yoga, I now bring over ten years of professional experience and personal study. My experience includes healing travel expeditions to such places as India, Africa, and South America, where I studied a broad range of stress management healing modalities, including yoga, Reiki, and indigenous healing techniques.

I have written a natural-living column in the New York *Daily News*, had TV lifestyle segments on *Home Matters* on the Discovery Network, NBC, and CBS, and taught corporate restorative yoga classes in such companies as Bayer, ABC Television Network, Ciba-Geigy, and Diversified Investment Services.

My experience as a yoga instructor has allowed me to observe closely, right from the yoga mat, the deep but often unacknowledged personal stress my students feel trying to meet the intense and ever-changing demands of living a twenty-first-century life.

YOUR PEACE URGE PROFILE

My yoga clients come from all walks of life. They're executives, single parents, nannies, judges, teachers, stockbrokers, CEOs of major corporations. But they all, in one way or another, express what I call the *peace urge*, the inner desire to find balance, to feel restored, to be happy and peaceful. When I discuss the *peace urge* in my classes, collective nods spread throughout the room. "I know what you mean," they seem to say.

Sound familiar? No doubt. Like a red flashing light at a

12. It's often hard for me to relax. ☐

13. I can't sit still—even so-called enjoyable
things such as watching a movie can be difficult. ☐

14. I feel pressured easily, even when my plate is
relatively clean. ☐

15. I never have time for myself. ☐

16. I often wish I could go on strike from my life
and stop shouldering so many responsibilities. ☐

17. When I'm distressed, I frequently say
nothing, build up steam, and then explode
either outwardly or inwardly, directly or
indirectly. ☐

18. I have trouble "giving" to myself, like allowing
myself a reward for a project well done at
work. ☐

19. I participate in some form of addictive
behavior (drinking, eating, spending, etc.) in
order to alleviate stress. ☐

20. I want to do everything perfectly. ☐

21. I sometimes feel physical manifestations of
stress such as heart palpitations, frequent
colds, headaches, or digestive disorders. ☐

Total number checked: _____

Your *Peace Urge* Profile can help you understand the extent to
which you are in or out of touch with your need for peace and
restoration. If you answered positively to more than 14 ques-

train crossing, your *peace urge* cautions you to stop. It tells you that you're going beyond your boundaries and that you're spent and have been carrying too heavy a load for too long. One of my clients told me that she felt as though her life was like a dried up well with no water in sight. That was her *peace urge* talking loud and clear. We know the *peace urge* intuitively. The desire to refuel spiritually and emotionally is innate. It signals that we're overextended and at a breaking point.

How strong is your *peace urge*? To help you assess its presence (or absence) in your life, consider each question below and check the box adjacent to the statements that apply to you, the ones in which "Yes, that's me" comes to mind.

1. I'm absentminded, and always feel rushed for no reason.
2. I have trouble engaging in quiet activities, such as reading a novel.
3. I need to be constantly on the go.
4. Sometimes I feel like I'm driven by a motor.
5. I'm chronically disorganized.
6. I always have something I should be doing or thinking about.
7. I'm a constant worrier.
8. I sometimes talk excessively.
9. I have trouble paying attention to details.
10. Listening and focusing on what others have say isn't my forte.
11. I never seem to have enough time in the day to get done what I need to.

tions, you have a strong *peace urge*—and it's far from satisfied. If your *peace urge* is moderate but still largely neglected, you answered 9 to 13 questions positively. If your *peace urge* is slight and only affects you occasionally because you're finding ways to satisfy it, you answered yes to 4 to 8 questions. Anything lower would indicate you have the urge for peace occasionally, but it's not a serious problem.

Based on your answers, you might be someone who experiences the *peace urge* less than you thought. Or you may have discovered that you have it frequently—perhaps having passed your symptoms off as other problems such as anxiety, nervousness, or work-related fatigue. If the latter applies to you, the Bliss Life Program can help.

The Bliss Life Program goes straight to the heart of self-care. It consists of three basic components, which can be done either separately or together to acknowdge your *peace urge* and to embrace your Bliss Principle, which I will discuss in detail in a moment.

The components of the Bliss Life Program include:

❧ *Bliss Breathing.*

The key component of the Bliss Life Program, also known as pranayama yoga, involves controlling the breath by consciously inhaling and exhaling using various breathing techniques. Bliss Breathing feeds the body with awareness, and helps clear the mind of distractions and stressors so that you can access the Bliss Principle.

✎ *The Relaxation Workout.*

The second component of the Bliss Life Program is a ten-step restorative yoga routine I created that you can do in just 20 to 25 minutes in the privacy of your home. I call it the Relaxation Workout. It's the same routine I teach to my students and clients that allows you to take more time to explore your Bliss Principle. To put it simply, the Relaxation Workout helps you access and experience your Bliss Principle through the body.

✎ *Lifestyle Tools for Transformation.*

The third component of the Bliss Life Program consists of lifestyle tools for transformation, which are simple environmental, self-care tips, and nutritious stress-free recipes that you can make and use to remember your Bliss Principle.

NOW IT'S YOUR TURN

This book will show you the components of my Bliss Life Program, how to access and live with your Bliss Principle, and how to use its healing energy to satisfy all aspects of your *peace urge*.

The Bliss Life Program is intimate. It's about tapping into you and taking recuperative moments throughout your day, whether you're at work, or in the comfort of your own home. You will find that as you embrace your Bliss Principle regularly through the Bliss Life Program, you will be empowered from within to optimize the challenges that inevitably come your way.

The Peace Urge, the Power of the Bliss Principle, and the Bliss Life Program

You are the same person for whom you are longing.

—YOGA MASTER RAMA OF HARIDWAR

AND KASHMIR (1900–1972)

According to Ayurveda (the "science of life"), India's traditional medicine, there are three unique blends of energy types in nature called *vata*, *pitta*, and *kapha*. Vata energy is quick and highly stimulating, pitta is grounding energy, and kapha is sluggish and slow moving. When one overpowers the other two, an energy imbalance ensues. Vata energy is prevalent in the twenty-first century; it keeps the mind busy, and the body constantly moving, breeding anxiety and fueling the *peace urge* in a big way. It makes the surface of our lives one busy blur.

Let me introduce you to John, a personal assistant to a CEO of a health company. An overachiever and perfectionist, John feels overwhelmed by the demands made of him at work. He is driven to do everything expected of him and more, and typically takes on a much larger share of responsibility than his coworkers. John is also a part-time college student, and determined to keep his GPA high.

The problem? John's life feels very stressful most of the time. I'll let him tell it in his own words:

> Sometimes my life gets so tiring that I don't know what to do. I find myself rushing all the time, and I can't sleep or eat. I feel chronically anxious and it always seems that there is too much to do and not enough time. Even though my body feels tired, I know I can't stop. I have to work, go to class, or take care of something. I have a huge craving for peace and think that if I could just slow down, I could enjoy all the good things in my life.

John's right. But it's all too easy to ignore our *peace urge* when we're distracted by the ticker tape of thoughts, worries, and the expanding to-do list that is constantly running through our minds.

Many of the *peace urges* we have arise because we ignore the stressful tension building in and around us over time. So often we just don't listen. We don't listen to our inner voice when it whispers to us, "Don't take that new position at the office! It will drain the life from you."

We also don't listen to our bodies when they tell us that we're tired down to our bones. Too often we push ourselves through the warning signals and ignore the stress we are feeling. This breeds and feeds the *peace urge* within us.

What happens when we ignore our stress? Many of my new clients tell me that they distract themselves by overeating, overspending, drinking, taking anxiety medication or sleep aids, or further overextending themselves.

It's vital for your well-being to listen to your urge for peace and to retreat from the world when you need to, even for just a few minutes here and there. In the long run, it can even save your life. Citing Ayurveda again, it is believed that denying the need for peace can cause a range of imbalances in the mind, body, and spirit, increasing the risk of diseases and ailments such as depression, cancer, insomnia, high blood pressure, and immune system dysfunctions. It's simply not healthy to ignore your *peace urge* for too long.

Recent scientific data concurs. According to researchers at Duke University Medical Center in Durham, North Carolina, for example, there is evidence that unmitigated, chronic stress (the *peace urge* denied) causes a hormonal chain of events that can ultimately contribute to heart disease, the nation's biggest killer for both men and women. Chronic stress can cause physiological changes that promote atherosclerosis—the slow buildup of plaque deposits in the arteries of the heart. Relatively minor stresses can also trigger significant cardiac abnormalities, such as myocardial ischemia, the condition in which the heart doesn't get enough blood. When our bodies are in a constant state of tension due to mental stress—ever ready to fight or flee—a host of physical problems result. As adrenaline courses through the body when it's really not needed, our blood pressure and our blood sugar are elevated, and the platelets in our blood become sticky and more likely to clot.

LONGING FOR ESCAPE

Your mind and body will put up with a great deal, but for many there eventually comes a time when the urge for peace becomes so strong that you are sent an undeniable message. Many of my clients wouldn't stop the frenzy of their stressful lifestyles until they were physically shut down by an illness, such as a debilitating cold or total exhaustion. One client, who was a successful partner at a high-powered New York City law firm, developed an intestinal ailment and could barely eat or sleep as a result of the ongoing stress and long hours demanded by her work. "My job is literally killing me," she told me. She eventually left the law profession to settle into a quieter, less stressful existence. One friend needed to be alerted by her eight-year-old that she was ignoring her *peace urge*. "Mommy, you have two black eyes. You need to rest," her daughter said, referring to the deep bags that had settled in on my friend's weary face after getting up too early and going to bed too late for several weeks.

The good news is that you don't need to make drastic changes to satisfy your *peace urge*. You don't need to quit your job, go on an exotic vacation, or spend a day at the local day spa. You don't even have to attend a formal yoga class to attain the sense of peace you seek.

I emphasize to my students that the calm, positive energy they get from taking my classes—the antidote for the *peace urge* we may be unaware we have—isn't confined to the yoga studio. The stillness, silence, and serenity that they experience during my yoga classes is at their disposal anytime, no matter where they are. It's inside each of us and ready to be accessed many times a day. It's what I call the Bliss Principle.

The Bliss Principle is a phrase I coined to describe the powerful wellspring of peaceful, restorative, healing energy we all possess. It's your center of peace, the remedy for the *peace urge* we may not be acknowledging in our twenty-first-century lifestyles. It's what I've witnessed as a student and instructor of yoga over the years.

The Bliss Principle is rooted in what is referred to in yoga scriptures as *Ananda*—bliss or supreme peace. According to

Kashmir Shavism, an ancient yoga philosophy, everything in the universe originates from what is called *spanda,* the supreme vibration or original pulsation of life itself.

It is said that spanda is filled with the qualities of blissful energy, divine love, and consciousness, and vibrates throughout the physical and nonphysical worlds.

The Bliss Principle stems from this supreme, blissful vibration and is the original peace that we can learn to recognize and experience within ourselves.

Yoga science states that bliss energy is actually housed in the heart region of the body, like a small "seedless white grape" of light. That's bliss described in a physical form. But bliss is also the spiritual state of awareness that yoga masters and gurus attain once they've reached the final goal of yoga called self realization, a state of oneness with one's own divinity.

But you don't have to be a yoga master to experience moments of your Bliss Principle. The Bliss Principle is with you wherever you go and is always ready to be accessed. It's with you when you do yoga, when you're sitting in traffic, and even when you're sick, unhappy, and seriously stressed out. Your Bliss Principle is a cache of centeredness and calm amid chaos. When we're in touch with it, we connect with supreme peace. Many of my students describe the physical sensation of the Bliss Principle they experience during classes as "liquid joy," "sweet tranquil rain," and "joyful happiness." It's the same kind of serenity you might feel during and after a yoga class or the endorphin-high you experience when you enter "the zone" during and after a good workout.

ACCESSING YOUR
BLISS PRINCIPLE

As you access your Bliss Principle it's important to know that it's not only a supremely peaceful energy that can help you feel restored, it's also a healing power. In his book *Quantum Healing*, Deepak Chopra, best-selling author and founder of the Chopra Center in Carlsbad, California, writes about the healing power of bliss. He concludes that when bliss is nurtured under the right conditions, bliss energy has been shown to alter heart rate, blood pressure, and hormone secretions in the body. He further states that bliss energy acts as a "mending force" that "bridges the physical and subtle worlds."

On a physiological level, your Bliss Principle is akin to the rest-and-digest response, which responds to our sense of equilibrium and is the opposite of the fight-or-flight response. When our rest-and-digest response is activated, our heart rate drops, blood pressure falls, and respiration slows and deepens. Blood flows to the core of the body, promoting good digestion, supporting the immune system, and infusing us with a sense of well-being.

Yet, it doesn't come to you on its own, like a pleasurable thought out of nowhere. You have to make a clearing for it, mentally and physically, by ridding yourself of stressful thoughts, mental chatter, and body tension. We can learn to intentionally incorporate small moments of healing and tranquility into our day. Whether these transformative moments last only a few seconds or several minutes, their effects are real and measurable—you'll see.

Clearly we can't eliminate stress. The potential for stress is always going to be a part of our lives, lurking behind every deadline, every obligation, every unexpected turn of events. But we can learn to manage stress, one breath at a time. The Bliss Life program, which will be described in detail in the following chapters, is designed to put you in touch with your Bliss Principle, which, although hidden, is always there to protect you from your own demanding lifestyle.

The Bliss Life Program is an inexpensive way to satisfy the *peace urge*. It's living-giving and, I believe, even life saving. Best of all, it's self-supportive, and that's very important. We can't always rely on experts to help us cope. In fact, with managed care's quick-fix mentality, many of us simply don't have that luxury. Twenty psychotherapy sessions, for example, are often the most a health plan will cover. Many of us are looking for a cost-effective, time-efficient, do-it-yourself paradigm. The Bliss Life Program is on the cutting edge of this growing trend and teaches tools that are easy to understand and easy to practice for a healthier, happier life.

Let's get started with one of the most important components of the Bliss Life Program: Bliss Breathing.

CHAPTER 2

Finding Your Bliss Principle Through Breath

Where there is no center of peace, bliss can never enter unintentionally.

— FOURTEENTH-CENTURY YOGA GURU JNANESHWAR MAHARAJ

*F*ar too many of us go through a lifetime never knowing what lies in the power of our breath and how we can access that power when we need it most. Thomas, an engineer in his early forties, for example, frequently experienced tension headaches when major projects were due at work. "Since I've started focusing on my Bliss Breathing, I don't get them nearly as often," he told me. Alice, an actress in her late twenties, relayed one day that she now used her Bliss Breathing to mentally prepare for auditions. "I used to get nervous and sweat profusely. Now, I breathe, breathe, breathe through it all and feel so much more control," she said.

Hidden to the physical eye, the breath contains the life force inside us. In yoga, the breath is the foundation of our energy and vitality. The more breath we can take in, especially when we're under pressure and stress, the better we are at sensing the presence of our Bliss Principle and our center of peace. Through conscious breathing, we can feel the enormous difference between stressful energy and peaceful energy.

Bliss Breathing is a direct pathway to our Bliss Principle, and it works to calm us in several ways. Rooted in the restorative practice of Pranayama yoga, Bliss Breathing helps reestablish our healthy breathing patterns, teaching us to consciously and systematically relax. It sets the rest-and-digest response in motion, the same one that is activated when we're in the throes of a hearty laugh or lost in a good book. In this instance, however, we're not waiting for it to be turned on by a pleasant or soothing experience. We're activating it from the bottom up, through breath.

On an even deeper level, deep, diaphragmatic breathing—Bliss Breathing—allows the lungs to fill with four to six times more oxygen than they take in during a shallow breath. Deep breathing slows the heart rate and also helps short-circuit the release of fight-or-flight hormones such as epinephrine (adrenaline), noradrenaline, and cortisol throughout the body.

In times of crisis or heightened stress, many of us have a tendency to breathe shallowly, which can actually work against us by enhancing anxiety and disrupting our ability to concentrate. In fact, shallow breathing and the stream of stress hormones the brain subsequently releases when we subconsciously experience feelings of fear or anger are the basis of the fight-or-flight response. This biochemical reaction to danger causes the heart to pump faster, blood pressure to shoot up, and blood vessels to redirect blood from the body's extremities to the muscles for greater strength.

The physical stress that results can lower the body's supplies of interferon and natural killer cells that are needed to help fight disease. Granted, the fight-or-flight response can be helpful if we're walking across a busy intersection in the path of an oncoming bus. But it's overkill, and perhaps even health threatening, when the stressors we're facing are ongoing and psychologically charged, such as running late for an important appointment because we're caught in traffic or juggling the competing demands of a busy job and running a family. If you think of it on a continuum, the fight or-flight response is at the opposite end from your Bliss Principle. Yet that highly revved up state is how many of us spend the majority of our waking hours.

Bliss Breathing, which involves deep, thorough inhalations (diaphragmatic breathing) followed by holding the breath on a deep inhalation, helps counteract the shallow chest breathing associated with stress.

Bliss Breathing also serves to ground us intellectually and can be useful when we're overly caught-up in a situation in which we need to distance ourselves. According to Herbert Benson, M.D., the Mind/Body Medical Institute associate professor of medicine at Harvard Medical School and the author of *The Relaxation Response*, relaxation techniques, such as restorative yoga practices like conscious breathing, "break the train of everyday thought." When you focus on your breath, you can momentarily stop paying attention to the stressful situation at hand, such as when you need to concentrate amid ringing telephones, hovering coworkers, and demanding clients. This is a situation one of my students, Patricia, a stockbroker, finds herself in daily. "When I focus on my breath, I can keep my cool and truly be productive. It's like going to the gym or giving myself a mental massage," she said.

Ginger, a client with a serious respiratory disorder, experienced vividly the healing power of her own breath.

Ginger arrived at our session carrying a portable oxygen tank because she often experienced shortness of breath. From the sound of her shallow breathing and her haggard expression, it was apparent that Ginger's health condition was causing not only physical discomfort but psychological stress. It also was clear that her *peace urge* was formidable.

I felt strongly that Ginger needed to learn to trust her own breathing again in order to alleviate her intense anxiety, which was debilitating both physically and psychologically. Let me emphasize that Ginger has a lung condition which requires medical treatment and which I was not attempting to cure. But I wanted to explore with Ginger how much of the anxiety and fatigue she experienced in association with her ailment was connected to how she thought about and experienced her breath. I wanted Ginger to break free of the mental baggage she carried about her condition by using the power of her own breath.

During Ginger's session, I initially had her lie in the Corpse Pose, a simple yoga posture in which she relaxed on her back with the focus on her breathing. We did this for twenty minutes. I then led her through a series of guided Bliss Breathing. With her eyes closed, I asked her to feel each breath as she inhaled and exhaled to feel the peace in it. My goal was for her to feel at ease with breathing and to feel its support, one breath at a time.

When our sixty minutes were up, Ginger's breathing pattern was even and deep. "I haven't felt this way for a long time," she said. She felt so comfortable that she actually forgot her portable oxygen tank when she left and had to return for it! Ginger was clearly not cured of her condition. But she had taken a measurable step toward breaking free of the stress that surrounded it.

BLISS BREATHING AND THE HEALING POWER OF THE BLISS PRINCIPLE

When we come to the threshold of the Bliss Principle through Bliss Breathing, healing can take place. We don't necessarily achieve a permanent healing, but we experience a measurable change that can last anywhere from a few minutes to an hour. The shift can be as subtle as a tight shoulder softening or a pleasantly uplifting feeling. No matter how small or large these transformations might feel to you, they have the power to provide what you need to balance your situation and can create the foundation for more substantive healing in the future.

When we alter our breathing so that it becomes deep and restorative, we experience the calming supremacy of the here and now.

It's a return to living with full awareness in the present. In yoga and other spiritual practices, it is believed that the present moment, rich with transformative powers, is all we really have. When nothing matters but the now, the experience is intimate and purifying.

The healing power of Bliss Breathing can help you through times of intense crisis as well. My sister's two-year bout with uterine cancer was a time when I needed to stay especially strong, to be there for her and to make it through her subsequent death. Being able to engage my center of peace through

Bliss Breathing during that process was a great comfort to me and was a way to support myself from the inside out.

One client, Louise, a forty-year-old mother of two, revealed that Bliss Breathing was what got her through a devastating divorce. It allowed her to find moments of inner calm, which helped fuel her courage to meet new people and begin a new life. "I'm just trying to remember to take one date at a time," she said. That's exactly the idea. You have to try little by little.

Accessing your innate supreme peace through Bliss Breathing doesn't happen immediately and requires real effort, especially in the beginning. But as you practice, it does get easier and more accessible. After even a little practice, those blissful moments become short spiritual journeys to tranquil places within. "When yet another catastrophe breaks out at work, I take a few measured breaths and I'm there," one client told me proudly, referring to her Bliss Principle.

BLISS BREATHING TECHNIQUE

So how do you engage your Bliss Principle through Bliss Breathing? It's easy. There are two basic components to Bliss Breathing: conscious deep breathing and breath retention.

Conscious deep breathing (also called three-part, diaphragmatic breathing) is simply breathing with awareness. To do it, focus on your breath as you inhale and exhale through your nose. On the inhalation, allow the breath to glide from the abdomen into the lungs and all the way up into the collarbone area. By simply paying attention to your breath, you're likely to experience an automatic calming effect. If you have a few moments now, try deep conscious breathing. Take two to ten deep breaths and just notice them. Close your eyes if you like. See if you feel a shift in your awareness. This is the first phase of creating a clearing for your Bliss Principle.

BLISS TIP:

To check if you're actually breathing from the depths of your diaphragm rather than shallowly from your chest, place your hand on your abdomen and watch as you feel it rise and fall in sync with each breath. Allow the breath to rise from the abdomen all the way up into your collarbones—and exhale out with ease. When you practice deep conscious breathing with awareness, you can feel your body and mind become centered and relaxed.

The second component of Bliss Breathing is breath retention, an ancient Pranayama yoga technique used to access higher states of consciousness and as preparation for meditation. The retention breath is done by holding your breath for a few seconds, then releasing with a controlled exhalation. You simply inhale through your nose, hold your breath on the count of one, two, then slowly exhale through your mouth with slightly parted lips. (You can also exhale through your nose if it's more comfortable for you.) This act of holding the breath acts as a big broom that gathers stress and tension collecting in the body. The exhalation sweeps those erosive emotions away, creating a clearing from which you can access your Bliss Principle. If you have a minute, try taking a retention breath or two. Inhale. Hold. Exhale. Try it again. Feel every muscle in your body, from head to toe, naturally relax as you relinquish your breath. Feel yourself engage your Bliss Principle. Feel the vibration shift. Do you feel as though you've just tuned into a more peaceful frequency, like finding the radio station with the clear classical music when you've been listening to static for too long?

In my classes, I take my students through a Bliss Breathing exercise, such as the one that follows, which combines both breathing techniques. Read through the steps before beginning. It might help if you record yourself slowly reading the steps aloud. That way you can listen to the instructions while you perform the steps for the first time. You'll need between 5 and 10 minutes to do this exercise.

Step 1: Sit upright and relaxed. Become aware of the present moment by consciously focusing on your breathing. The key word here is consciously. Remember to experience your breathing. Just notice it.

Step 2: Begin taking deep, conscious breaths in and out through your nose. Imagine filling yourself with life-giving oxygen from your belly button all the way to the top of your collarbones. Then exhale "long," as I like to say, through your nose. As you inhale and exhale through your nose, stay focused on the sound and feel of each breath. You're creating the clearing to connect with your Bliss Principle.

Step 3: Close your eyes, if you can (you may not be able to do so if you're in public), and as you continue to focus on your breathing, feel the stillness and silence in your body. Continue to follow your breath with awareness for 30 seconds.

Step 4: Take a retention breath. With your eyes still closed, inhale and hold the breath for two seconds, then slowly exhale through your mouth with slightly parted lips. Feel your muscles relax as you complete the exhale. Then continue taking deep, oxygenated, conscious breaths for 30 seconds.

Step 5: Take another retention breath by inhaling and holding the breath for 2 seconds, then slowly exhaling through your mouth. Then continue taking deep, oxygenated, conscious breaths for 30 seconds. Deep, conscious breathing is your default mode.

Step 6: Take your final retention breath by inhaling and holding the breath for 2 seconds, then slowly exhaling through your mouth. Then continue taking deep, oxygenated, conscious breaths for 30 seconds.

Step 7: Finally, open your eyes and breathe naturally without too much focus. Gently gaze at any still object before you that catches your eye, such as your hands, legs, or feet, a tree, the ground, or a wall, and feel the stillness and silence in that body part or object for a moment.

How do you feel? Do you feel expansiveness inside you? Do you sense an energy that is still, tranquil, and free? I hope so. This is your supreme peace, your Bliss Principle, coming into your awareness. Stay with this sensation as long as you can and let the vibration saturate your body.

After you've done this Bliss Breathing exercise, you may feel spacey and pleasantly detached. Some of my students say they're "floating." This is natural. Think of it as the energy given off by your Bliss Principle. Nonetheless, when you're done, it's important to ground yourself to create a feeling of closure. When you complete the exercise, stand up and feel your feet. Stand in the yoga position called the tree pose. Simply stand with your feet shoulder-width apart and feel your entire body supported as you become rooted into the soles of your feet. Do this for a few moments before you resume any activity.

I recommend that you do not attempt Bliss Breath-

ing while driving, taking any prescription drugs that cause drowsiness, or engaging in any activity that requires you to be alert to your surroundings.

ADDING MANTRA AND MUSIC TO THE MIX

Repeating a mantra (a spiritually charged word) or using an uplifting phrase regularly is a highly beneficial yoga practice. Why? Because words have the power to transform. They can still the mind, still the body, and create a new reality in a moment. Words can take you from angry to happy in a split second.

While you're practicing your Bliss Breathing, especially during intense circumstances such as a stressful situation at work, try silently repeating calm and reassuring phrases to yourself such as "I'm going to be okay. I can solve this problem," or "cool, relaxed mind, calm body," after each retention breath. For some, the combination of the two—Bliss Breathing and mantra—is especially soothing. If you go this route, make sure your inner voice is continuously supportive. If a negative, beat-yourself-up voice chimes in, such as "I can't do this; I'm in over my head," drown it out. Say "no" to yourself, and then keep repeating your positive supportive statements to stay on track.

Another option is to repeat a power word, such as "peace" or "calm." While saying it to yourself, continue to focus and do your Bliss Breathing. By combining your Bliss Breathing and your power word you amplify your experience of the Bliss Principle. Using a power word like "calm" can be a cue to engage your Bliss Breathing right after an intensely stressful day or encounter.

In lieu of or in addition to a power word, you might also try music with sounds from nature, such as ocean waves or instrumental string music without lyrics. I personally love the sounds of world-renowned sitar player Ravi Shankar. The Indian stringed instrument, the sitar, draws the mind to silence through its soothing sound. Background music while doing your Bliss Breathing helps create a calm mood and can amplify the effects of deep conscious breathing.

BLISS TIP:

Yet another technique you might try is to close your eyes and picture yourself bathed in a blue light while concentrating on your breathing. Blue, a healing color in Buddhist medicine, is considered energizing. For other suggestions on stress-reduction techniques that might work especially well for you, see Chapter 6, Personalizing Your Bliss Life Program.

Don't be surprised if your Bliss Principle feels inaccessible at first. Some of my newer students report finding it difficult, for example, to ignore outside distractions, like the fire truck that howls during our sessions or the construction workers hammering on the sidewalk just outside the building. "I can't stop thinking about what I'm going to make for dinner," another confessed. "Relax and keep breathing," I told her. Your desire for peace is just as important as the act of Bliss Breathing itself. You have to be strong in your intention to access the peace inside your soul. If the will is there, the peace will be there for you, but you must create a clearing for it to take root.

If initially you feel like you just don't "get" Bliss Breathing and can't seem to escape the mental chatter, I urge you to hang in there and keep practicing. Bliss Breathing is simple, but with all the competition from the outside world, you may need to take some solid practice time to learn. It's a skill you develop. As long as you combine intention with awareness and breathe deeply from the diaphragm, you'll find that you can access a feeling of calm and balance even when confronted with an unpleasant situation. You'll also become astute at noticing the opposite—when you breathe shallowly from your chest, anxiety and muscle tightness develop and your mind begins to race and spin.

Bliss Breathing is with you all the time, wherever you are. You can do your Bliss Breathing while you're getting a manicure, when you're watching TV, at the beach, sitting at your computer, or before your morning commute—and because it's not obvious, nobody has to know. Ideally, it's best to be in a quiet room, but that's not essential. In fact, you often need the power of Bliss Breathing the most when silence is unavailable, such as in a bustling office or your own noisy kitchen.

CREATING A CLEARING WITH MEDITATION

Meditation is another component of the Bliss Life Program and goes quite naturally with Bliss Breathing. Meditation helps to still the mind and temporarily silence the chatter of stressful thoughts so that you are able to feel the Bliss Principle vibration, both during and after meditation.

It is said that stress originates in the mind and settles in the body. I have seen how our stressful thoughts exhaust us and lead to the *peace urges* we experience. In yoga, it is thought that our minds are naturally meant to mimic the periods of rest and relaxation our bodies require to restore our organs. Meditation scholars and masters tend to prescribe regular daily acts of meditation so the mind and body can rest and recharge.

The act of meditation can feel like taking a brief pilgrimage to tranquil places within.

While teaching meditation to a group of women in prison, it always amazed me how just a few minutes of meditation seemed to give them an inner freedom unrestrained by the prison bars around them. It was clear from their serene faces that they had tapped into a center of peace, a place far beyond their confinement.

MEDITATION TIPS TO ACCESS THE BLISS PRINCIPLE

PLACE AND TIME:

▸ Find a quiet place clear of any external distractions.

▸ First thing in the morning or at the end of the busy day are the best times.

▸ Give yourself at least 5 to 20 minutes to meditate and be quiet.

POSTURE AND BREATH:

▸ Sit in a chair or in a yogi cross-legged position on the floor.

▸ Use pillows to support you as needed.

▸ Now bring your attention to your breath.

▸ Do two Bliss Breaths and allow yourself to be relaxed and become centered as you sit in stillness.

▸ Go back to normal breathing.

CHOOSE A POWER WORD:

▸ Now, think of a word that brings peace to your mind (e.g., love, peace, tranquility, silence, etc.). This will focus you and help to quiet your mind even more.

CLOSE YOUR EYES AND CONCENTRATE ON YOUR BREATH AND POWER WORD:

▸ Now, close your eyes and focus your awareness on your breath and power word.

▸ Say your power word to yourself quietly while remaining aware of your breathing.

▸ If thoughts interfere, gently refocus on your power word and your breathing.

RELAX IN THE DARKNESS:

▸ With eyes closed, relax into the stillness and silence of the darkness before you for at least 3 to 5 minutes to start.

▸ When you've had enough, gently open your eyes.

▸ Take a Bliss Breath and relax for a few moments.

▸ Feel the vibration of peace in and around you. Allow the vibration to saturate your mind, body, and spirit. Allow it to become a part of who you are.

▸ Before you resume outer activity, ground yourself by rocking back and forth into the soles of your feet.

BLISS TIP:

Support Tools for Meditating:

1. Quiet corner to sit for meditation
2. Meditation pillow for back support
3. Meditation shawl to keep warm
4. Meditation oil (sandalwood and frankincense are recommended)
5. Meditation music (string and drum instruments)
6. A hand-size quartz crystal to hold (optional)

CHAPTER 3

The Relaxation Workout: Finding Your Bliss Principle Through the Body

Here in this body are the sacred rivers: here are the sun and moon as well as all the pilgrimage places. I have not encountered another temple as blissful as my own body.

— SARAHA

*B*liss Breathing and meditation are two powerful tools you have at your fingertips to help satisfy your *peace urge* and to invoke your innate peace vibration.

But when both are combined with restorative hatha yoga postures, what I call Bliss Moves, a whole physical dimension opens to experience the Bliss Principle.

Bliss Moves create clearing in the body by flushing out the stagnant energy blocked by stress. In my restorative yoga workshops and classes, I escort my clients through a series of Bliss Moves that I call the Relaxation Workout, which is a full 60 minutes of restorative yoga postures combined with Bliss Breathing.

In this chapter, I'll present a 20 to 25 minute version of this workout that you can do in the privacy of your home, at a spa party you host for a group of friends, on vacation, or even at the office in a conference room that's not being used. My Relaxation Workout features a select combination of ten restorative Bliss Moves for relaxation, healing, and restoration.

The Relaxation Workout helps us to consciously relax. Each Bliss Move creates an internal environment for relaxation, and with it a clearing inside the body that helps us surrender to the peace inside. The power of the relaxed state allows you to let go of stress, tension, and worries about the future, and summons the Bliss Principle energy.

As with Bliss Breathing, the Relaxation Workout leads to small and large transformations. In my yoga classes, I see tight smiles loosen, stiff bodies unwind, tired eyes turn into tranquil pools—and that's after just one session. This is because so much of the stress we feel gets stored in the body. According to yoga science, there are 72,000 subtle nerves, or *nadis*, in the body, all situated in the spinal column. These nadis are passageways for the life force to nourish all the systems of the body. When your system is under stress, these nadis become blocked and tension gets locked in muscles and joints in the neck, back, and shoulders, resulting in physical tightness, fatigue, and often pain.

Before a yoga class or private session it's not unusual for me to hear someone complain about one part of their body that seems to hold on to their stress. As one client put it, "It's as though a ton of weights is digging into my shoulder."

Bliss Moves work on a deep, physical level to soothe the nervous system and disable the fight-or-flight response by freeing areas where energy is blocked and releasing it through a combination of breathing, stretching, and focusing.

The restorative yoga postures you'll do in this routine have many lasting benefits. They can help to stabilize the heart rate and restore lung capacity to its full potential, while also promoting balance, strength, flexibility, and skeletal alignment. Bliss Moves teach us to stretch our bodies beyond the tenseness we feel. We often let the tension in our joints and muscles trap us so that we feel caged rather than supported by our bodies. Stretching can alleviate that tension so that our bodies feel graceful and fluid again.

Stretching not only feels good, it physically encourages the development of elongated, supple muscles. It also helps restore flexible joints, making them stronger and less prone to injury. Restorative yoga uses the benefits of stretching to promote healthy circulation and to stimulate lymphatic flow, the body's system for eliminating toxins.

The restorative postures I feature in the Relaxation Workout are simple and easy to learn. They include:

> Corpse Pose with Deep Conscious Breathing (known as Savasana in yoga tradition).
>
> Yoga Nidra (Tensing and Releasing).
>
> Child Pose (Balasana).
>
> Cat Cow Stretch.
>
> Downward Dog (Adho Mukha Svanasana).
>
> Crocodile Pose (Makarasana).
>
> Body Extension Stretch (Salabhasana).
>
> Body Scan.
>
> The Comfortable Cross-Legged Position (Sukhasana).
>
> The Butterfly Mudra.

If these poses aren't familiar to you, they soon will be as you perform the workout. You will probably even have a favorite or two. The Relaxation Workout is for all ages. However, it does require a strong back as well as flexible and sturdy wrists and knees to move in and out of each posture. To play it safe, consult a physician before beginning the Relaxation Workout if you've had major surgeries, have chronic issues involving your lower back, wrists, and knees, if you're being treated for high blood pressure or depression, or are pregnant.

While doing your Relaxation Workout, make sure you're not exerting yourself. If you're straining, you're not doing restorative yoga. Instead, try to be steady and comfortable while doing each posture. Relax and maintain awareness of your breathing during all the postures.

Avoid holding your breath when performing the postures, unless you're instructed to do so. You will take restorative rests between each posture as you go through the routine, and will be asked to do Bliss Breathing at strategic points throughout.

WORKOUT PREPARATION

Before you get started, here are a few tips to keep in mind to help you get the most out of the Relaxation Workout.

❦ *Create a supportive environment.*

No matter where you are when you decide to do your Relaxation Workout, it's important that the space be clean, quiet, and safe. Creating an environment to support your Relaxation Workout is always good, because it promotes the process of becoming relaxed. Let's face it, clutter and noise can be distracting, even stress inducing, in and of themselves. It's also best to do your Relaxation Workout in a well-ventilated room. You will be doing plenty of breathing during your workout, so, to assure that your lungs get clean air, I suggest slightly opening a window for fresh air to circulate.

❦ *Wear comfortable clothing.*

Wear loose-fitting, breathable clothing while doing your Relaxation Workout. This will enable you to move easily in and out of each posture. It's also good to have a pair of socks and sweater nearby in case you get a chill. Use a thick yoga mat or towel. To assure your comfort, I recommend using a double-padded, sticky yoga mat, but a cushy towel or exercise mat will also do. You can also have a few throw pillows around to support you while meditating or lying on your back.

❦ *Try not to eat heavily.*

Hold off on eating or drinking heavily for at least 45 minutes before doing your Relaxation Workout. Follow the same eating routine you would use when you're about to work out at the gym. A heavy stomach while doing the Relaxation Workout might put you to sleep. It can also be uncomfortable, which can interfere with accessing your Bliss Principle.

BLISS TIP:

To further create a mood, you might start your Relaxation Workout with a prayer, or by burning mood-relaxing incense such as Champa (my favorite) or frankincense, or even lighting a lavender aromatherapy candle. To establish a tranquil atmosphere, you can also play soothing music or recordings of nature sounds like the ocean crashing against the shore or falling rain. Just be sure to choose music that truly resonates with you.

THE RELAXATION WORKOUT

Take a minute to read through the workout before beginning so that you are familiar with the poses. Even better, make a recording of yourself reading the workout, then play it back and do the workout according to your own verbal instructions.

Special Note: Take a moment between each posture to absorb the silence and feel the energetic power of each position. Feel the expansion that occurs in your body with each Bliss Move posture. Allow your body to relax into this expansion. You've created a clearing for The Bliss Principle. In addition, take only one Bliss Breath (do one count of

deep breathing and a retention breath) between each
completed posture as you lie in stillness.

❦ Bliss Move 1: Corpse Pose with Deep Conscious Breathing (Figure 1)

Bliss Principle Healing Benefits: This pose, considered
one of total relaxation, calms the brain and helps relieve
stress. It's also thought to ease mild depression, headaches,
fatigue, and insomnia, and help lower blood pressure.

Figure 1

Step 1: To start, lie on your back and close your eyes.
Allow your arms to comfortably rest at your sides with your
palms facing up. Allow your feet to naturally turn out and
let the weight of your head, shoulders, back, pelvis, and legs
melt down into the floor.

Step 2: Bring your awareness to your breath; follow each
breath as you inhale and as you exhale.

Step 3: Next, allow yourself to be in the present moment
with each breath you take. Feel your breathing as it flows in
and out like a wave in the ocean. As you exhale, follow the
wave as it is drawn out to sea, and again follow as it returns
to shore while you inhale. Let each body part relax with
each breath you take. Do this for 3 minutes, basking

in the peaceful sensation, before moving on to Bliss
Move 2.

❧ Bliss Move 2:
Yoga Nidra (Figure 2)

Bliss Principle Healing Benefits: This Bliss Move clears
out stagnant energy and tension in the limbs and body. It
takes the Corpse Pose to a deeper level by engaging the
body in tensing and relaxing each key area in order to
release stress in that area.

Figure 2

While still in the Corpse Pose, go from head to toe
tensing and releasing your muscles in each body part as
directed below. (Note: *Gently* tense each body part; try not
to strain in any way. Go easy on your body.)

Step 1: Bring awareness to the face. Gently tense your
entire face with one big frown. Tense your mouth, eyes, lips,
cheeks, and forehead all at the same time for a few seconds
and then relax your entire face. Close your eyes. Take a
retention breath (hold for a count of two, then release the
breath) and then resume normal conscious breathing.
Relax. Gently open your eyes.

Step 2: Bring awareness to the neck. Gently roll your
head from side to side, tensing the muscles in your neck for

a few seconds. Return your head to center and relax the neck area completely. Take a retention breath and then resume normal conscious breathing.

Step 3: Bring awareness to the shoulders. Leaving your arms on the floor, lift your shoulders and squeeze them together in front of your chest. Squeeze and relax. Then squeeze your shoulders up toward your ears and relax. Take a retention breath and then resume normal conscious breathing.

Step 4: Bring your awareness to both of your arms and make fists of both hands. Tighten the muscles in your arms and raise them slightly off the floor; then lower your arms and allow them to melt into the floor. Relax. Take a retention breath and then resume normal conscious breathing.

Step 5: Bring your awareness to your abdomen area. Tighten your stomach muscles for a few seconds, then relax the area. Take a retention breath and then resume normal conscious breathing and relax a bit more.

Step 6: Bring awareness to the buttocks by squeezing the buttock muscles tight. Try to raise them slightly off the floor for a few seconds, then relax the buttocks and let them sink into the floor. Take a retention breath and resume normal conscious breathing.

Step 7: Bring awareness to both legs. Squeeze and tighten the muscles in both legs for a few seconds, starting in your calves and moving all the way up into your thighs. Then release the tension. Relax the legs; allow them to melt into the floor beneath you. Follow with a retention breath and resume conscious breathing. Relax for a few moments. Using your awareness, sense the peaceful shift building inside you. Now, go on to Bliss Move 3.

BLISS TIP:

If you're having trouble relaxing when you do the Relaxation Workout, just follow the flow of your breath. As you inhale and exhale, imagine your breath to be the ebb and flow of the ocean. As you breathe in, waves roll softly to the sandy shore. As you breathe out, they retreat into the deep taking all anxiety with them. You're fully in the moment, letting go while getting in touch with your Bliss Principle, the natural peace you were born with and to which you're entitled.

☙ **Bliss Move 3: Child Pose** (Figure 3)

Bliss Principle Healing Benefits: This pose creates a clearing for your center of peace by releasing tension in the lower back and tightness in the shoulder blades, and soothes the nervous system as well.

Figure 3

Step 1: Keeping your awareness on the breath, come onto your hands and knees, with your shoulders vertically above your wrists and with your hips above your knees. Relax the tops of your feet on the floor (don't flex them).

Step 2: Bring your buttocks toward your heels and your belly button toward your thighs while you stretch your arms out in front you. Feel the stretch in your spine, and rest your forehead on the mat or on a pillow and relax as you take four consecutive conscious *deep* breaths, inhaling and exhaling through your nose. Hold this position for about 1 minute.

Now go on to Bliss Move 4.

❦ Bliss Move 4: Cat Cow Stretch
(Figures 4a–4c)

Bliss Principle Healing Benefits: The Cat Cow Stretch creates a clearing by freeing the body of tension and realigning the spine. In yoga tradition, the spine is sacred. It is where our primary nerves in the body are stored and plays an important role in the vitality and rejuvenation of the body.

Figure 4a

When we're holding stress in the spine, we prevent access of the spinal nerves to key organs in the body.

Step 1: Come onto your hands and knees and align your knees directly under your hips with your fingers facing forward and your hands directly under your shoulders.

Step 2: As you inhale, drop your belly toward the floor and raise your head back slightly toward your buttocks

(Figure 4a). Gently push through your hands and knees and feel an invigorating stretch in the front of your body and

Figure 4b

spine.

Step 3: As you exhale, go in the opposite direction. Point your toes and round your back and entire spine, tucking in your tailbone. Draw your chin to your chest. (Be sure to pull in your abdomen while exhaling.) Feel the gentle stretch in the spine (Figure 4b). Repeat the Cat Cow Stretch four times in a row consecutively (do it with eyes closed if you feel comfortable; it adds a wonderful feeling to the pose). Rest back into Child Pose (Figure 4c) and relax for 30 seconds following your breathing—feel the peaceful expansion before moving on to Bliss Move 5.

Figure 4c

❦ Bliss Move 5: Downward Facing Dog
(Figures 5a–5d)

Bliss Principle Healing Benefits: This move brings fresh blood to the heart, invigorating the entire body, and creates a clearing for your center of peace by eliminating tension in the hamstrings and shoulders. **Note: Do not hold your breath while doing this Bliss Move. Keep breathing and be aware of inhaling and exhaling through your nose.**

Figure 5a

Step 1: Come onto your hands and knees. Your arms and shoulders should be in alignment with your wrists, and your knees in alignment with your hips (Figure 5a).

Step 2: Now tuck your toes under and arch your lower back in one complete movement and lift your knees off the floor. Straighten your legs and arms and relax your chin. Make your neck long and soft. Keep your spine long and the hips lifted up. Feel a nice stretch through the spine, arms, and legs as you look back toward your big toes.

Figure 5b

Hold your arms steady and strong with head centered as your arms stay parallel to your ears. Avoid collapsing your shoulders (Figure 5b).

Step 3: Now, drop your heels down toward the floor and feel a nice stretch behind your legs as you relax into the pose. Hold the pose and maintain deep breathing for 10 seconds. Come out of the pose sooner if you feel a need to.

Figure 5c

Step 4: Come back onto your hands and knees (Figure 5c) and return to the Child Pose (Figure 5d); rest for 30 seconds and follow the breath before moving on to Bliss Move 6.

Figure 5d

❧ *Bliss Move 6: Crocodile Pose* (Figure 6)

Bliss Principle Healing Benefits: This Bliss Move soothes the nervous system and clears tension in the lower back. It creates a clearing for your Bliss Principle by emphasizing relaxation and awareness of the breath.

Figure 6

Step 1: Come out of Child Pose and lie on your stomach with your arms folded at head level.

Step 2: Place your forehead comfortably on folded arms and rest.

Step 3: Observe the rising and falling of your abdomen as it expands and contracts with each breath. Feel yourself become more and more relaxed with each breath you take, as you connect with the stillness of the floor. Do this for 3 minutes. Feel the peaceful vibrations in your body as you rest. Then move on to Bliss Move 7.

❦ Bliss Move 7: Body Extension Stretch
(Figures 7a–7c)

Bliss Principle Healing Benefits: This Bliss Move energetically tones the nervous system and vital organs and creates a space for your center of peace by clearing tension and releasing stagnant energy throughout the body.

Figure 7a

Step 1: While lying on your stomach, bring your arms straight out in front of you and bring your head forward with your chin to the mat and look out in front of you (Figure 7a).

Figure 7b

Step 2: Now raise your upper and lower body together slightly off the ground into a lifted stretch. Hold the stretch from the base of your spine and the center of the body. You should feel tautness from your center connecting the upper and lower part of the body. Hold the lifted stretch for 3 to 5 seconds (Figure 7b).

Figure 7c

Step 3: Slowly, with control, bring both your upper and lower body simultaneously back down to the floor.

Step 4: Rest back into the Crocodile Pose, on your stomach with your head rested on your arms (Figure 7c). Relax for 30 seconds. Then repeat one more time before moving on to Bliss Move 8.

❧ *Bliss Move 8: Body Scan* (Figure 8)

Bliss Principle Healing Benefits: This Bliss Move is therapeutic for the nerves throughout your entire body, and integrates breath into areas of the body stiffened by stress.

In fact, I often remind my students to try not to fall asleep during this exercise (it's that relaxing).

Figure 8

Step 1: Gently roll onto your back into the Corpse Pose and follow your breath as it goes in and out of your lungs. Experience the peaceful vibration emerging.

Step 2: As you do this Bliss Move, you'll lead yourself through a guided tour of your body. As you inhale, direct your breath to each targeted body part. As you exhale, relax that area of the body.

Arms: As you inhale, imagine your arms filling with breath, then exhale slowly and relax your arms.

Shoulders: As you inhale, imagine your shoulders filling with breath, then exhale slowly and relax your shoulders.

Neck: As you inhale, imagine your neck filling with breath, then exhale slowly and relax your neck.

Stomach: As you inhale, imagine your stomach filling with breath, then exhale slowly and relax your stomach.

Chest: As you inhale, imagine your chest filling with breath, then exhale slowly and relax your chest.

Face: As you inhale, imagine your face filling with breath, then exhale slowly and relax your face.

Top of Your Head: As you inhale, imagine the top of your head filling with breath, then exhale slowly and relax the top of your head. Finally, bring your awareness back to normal breathing and relax for 30 seconds.

Feel the Bliss Principle emerge in your body and mind, and soak in the energy for a minute or so before moving gently on to Bliss Move 9.

❦ Bliss Move 9: Comfortable Cross-Legged Position (Sukhasana) in Meditation Posture (Figure 9)

Bliss Principle Healing Benefits: This pose creates a center of peace by clearing the mind of busy thoughts, and helps to heal the immune system from stress overload.

Figure 9

Step 1: Bring yourself up into a cross-legged position. (You can use a chair if you have trouble sitting in this position.) While sitting allow your hands to rest in your lap or on top of each knee.

Step 2: Gently close your eyes.

Step 3: Sit in stillness. Follow your breath in and out, one breath at a time with each inhalation and exhalation. If thoughts come up, ignore them and keep your awareness on your breath. Sit this way for 2 minutes. If you have more time, feel free to sit for up to 15 minutes.

Step 4: Slowly come out of mediation, open your eyes, and relax for one minute. Last, do one round of Bliss Breathing.

Bliss Breathing refresher: Take a couple of deep conscious breaths, then hold the breath on the inhale for 2 seconds (breath retention) from the throat area, then exhale out long and slow through parted lips, allowing the entire body to relax even more. Resume normal breathing.

Feel the power of your Bliss Principle—your innate center of peace, your original peace vibration—bubbling over into your awareness and body. When you are ready, go ahead and move on to Bliss Move 10. If you feel you need to stretch your legs out, feel free to shake them out now, then return to a cross-legged position.

☙ Bliss Move 10: The Butterfly Mudra
(Figures 10a–10g)

Figure 10a

Bliss Principle Healing Benefits: This final Bliss Move fosters stillness and silence throughout the mind, body, and spirit.

The Butterfly Mudra completes the Relaxation Workout. In Yoga terms, *mudra* means "seal." In other words, a mudra seals the subtle, healing energies and benefits of the Relaxation Workout in and around the body.

Figure 10b

Figure 10c

Figure 10d

Step 1: While still in a cross-legged sitting position (or in a chair), bring your palms together into prayer position at the heart region. Then close your eyes and slowly raise your hands in prayer position above your head with your arms up alongside your ears (Figures 10a, 10b).

Step 2: Stretch your arms out through your fingertips; try to get a nice stretch through your arms. As you reach toward the infinite sky, consciously breathe deeply; do this for 5 seconds (Figure 10c).

Step 3: Now release your arms slowly, as if a butterfly, with palms down. Slowly let your arms release

Figure 10e

Figure 10f

as they flow down (inch by inch) until your fingertips softly touch the floor (Figures 10d–10f). Now, repeat the Butterfly Mudra two more times, consectively, doing a total of 3 Butterfly Mudras back to back starting in the prayer position (Figure 10g). Afterward, bring your hands back to your lap and slowly open your eyes. You have just completed the Relaxation Workout. Enjoy the deep relaxation and invigorating energy you're experiencing. This is your Bliss Principle.

Figure 10g

BLISS TIP:

Give yourself a good half hour or more to do the Relaxation Workout so you can bask in the quiet blissful moment afterward. The workout can be done before you start your day, at lunchtime, or when you get home from work. Feel the vibration within you. Sense where you were before the Relaxation Workout and feel the frequency shift that has occurred in your mind and body.

MODIFYING YOUR
BLISS MOVES

In my classes, I often take my clients, especially those who are overly stressed by work or a medical condition, on more extended journeys with the Relaxation Workout, sometimes having them spend as much as 20 to 30 minutes practicing on just their Bliss Breathing or a particular Bliss Move, to ignite their Bliss Principle. If you have more time occasionally, I encourage you to do so as well. You might even want to concentrate on one or two Bliss Moves that focus on relieving stress where you feel it most in your body. It's fine to personalize the workout, if you like, and focus on your favorites or those you feel provide you with the most benefit. (More on that in Chapter 6.)

Adding Aroma Oil for Calmness

The right aroma can help jump-start your Relaxation Workout or complete it as you absorb the therapeutic benefits it provides. A whiff or a dab on the wrist points with the right aroma oils can lead to a richer experience. Just make sure you wash your hands after applying to avoid irritating the eyes.

What Scent to Use

Lavender, mandarin orange, lemon, ylang ylang, and sandalwood are great aromas for soothing tense muscles and calming the mind.

How often should you do the workout? It's up to you. In general, I recommend doing the Relaxation Workout at least once a week to support your Bliss Breathing, which you may be doing throughout your day. The Workout is an effective way to reinforce the presence of your Bliss Principle, ease your *peace urge* challenges, and will help keep the fight-or-flight response in check when the conditions are less than life threatening. The Relaxation Workout is an experience you'll want to treat yourself to again and again when you have extra time.

CHAPTER 4

Lifestyle Tools for Remembering the Bliss Principle

The soul is a garden enclosed, our own perpetual
paradise where we can be refreshed and restored.

—Thomas Moore

If you've been practicing your Bliss Breathing and doing the Bliss Relaxation Workout regularly, you're probably already feeling better and in more control over any emotional stress you may be having. More important, you may be becoming more aware of the inner presence of your Bliss Principle as tangible internal energy waiting to support you and offer you a peaceful transformation when you need it most.

Still, as part of my Bliss Life Program, there's another component available to you that can help you satisfy your *peace urge* and access your center of peace, one breath at a time, called tools for transformation. Unlike practicing Bliss Breathing and the Bliss Moves I suggest in my workout, tools for transformation are Bliss Maintenance, which work from the outside in, rather than the inside out, to maintain the awareness of your Bliss Principle.

The premise of Bliss Maintenance is the idea that the environment we create for ourselves in our home and/or workplace and the little nurturing things we do for ourselves can reinforce the presence of our center of peace. Some tools provide visual and other sensory cues that can trigger a sense of peace just by their presence. Other approaches evoke rejuvenation through the thoughtful action they require. The intention of each tool is to support, comfort, and soothe you, and to act as a reminder that there is an innate peaceful energy within us, a tranquil vibration that is a part of life itself.

Many of my clients are amazed by how these small alterations can create seismic shifts in their psyche. I think you'll be surprised by the quiet and controlled moments of reflection they can help you create for yourself, even amidst a hectic schedule with ongoing pressures. Here are some of my favorites.

THE BLISS PRINCIPLE:

It satisfies your *peace urge*. It's your innate center of peace—a deep wellspring of stillness, silence, serenity, freedom, expansion, tranquility, joy, and calmness. It's internal spiritual energy you can access at will that lives as part of your life force. It resonates with a wide spectrum of peaceful qualities. It's there when you need to retreat and feel relieved of stress and other pressures through the relaxation techniques in this book. It's with you wherever you go—at the supermarket, at work, on vacation, at the doctor's office.

CREATE A TRANQUILITY ALTAR

One of the first things you can do is to create a tranquility altar—a designated three-dimensional center of peace that becomes a physical reminder of your Bliss Principle. It can be large or small. Its purpose is to honor all that is peaceful and calm, and to signify that peace is important to your life. A tranquility altar can also be a functional space where you do your Bliss Breathing, say prayers, and contemplate your day. It can serve as a reminder to reflect and let yourself become replenished by its pure color and beauty. Think of a tranquility altar as natural feng shui—the ancient Chinese practice using the artful placement of objects that hold meaning and energy (chi) to alter one's state of mind—but without all the fuss.

I was taken with the idea of a tranquility altar a few years ago while staying in India at an ashram—a place where one goes on spiritual retreat to do self-inquiry practices such as meditation. Dotted throughout the ashram were *pujas* (tranquility altars), or designated places of worship. Each puja glowed with beauty and featured a special arrangement of alluring flowers placed on an exquisite silk cloth, along with a brilliant candle. I couldn't resist stopping to take in the beauty and the calmness each puja emanated. Each was a reminder that peace exists inside me and can be accessed through simple but beautiful surroundings.

Many of my clients are initially skeptical about creating a tranquility altar. Some think it sounds too new agey, or that it won't work for them. Some feel that they just don't have space for it in their house. I've heard this argument a lot. In fact, you don't need a room of your own or even much space to accommodate an altar. A spare corner, a cranny, or counter space somewhere will do. I urge my clients to move those papers, boxes, and knickknacks, and claim that little area for their own.

To create a tranquility altar, you'll need a collection of symbolic objects that are associated with peace. You can use almost anything that calls out to you, but here are four basic elements I recommend.

❧ A tray, mat, or silk puja cloth.

For safety and aesthetic reasons, the foundation of your tranquility altar is just as important as the objects you place on it. You want a surface that won't be flammable but will reflect the unique quality of your altar. A beautiful wooden or bamboo tray, a ceramic mat or a patterned silk puja cloth (a specially made double-sided and padded silk cloth) all serve well. Please remember if you use a puja cloth that you should never leave your altar unattended when a candle is lit.

❧ Candle:

Since ancient times, the symbolic meaning of a candle flame has been a "bridge" between the spiritual and the earthly realms. A candle is the centerpiece of your tranquility altar and acts as the focal point. The color of the candle holds symbolic meaning, so you may want to choose it carefully. White, for example, signifies purification or peace; violet/indigo signifies spirituality; yellow, happiness and joy; orange, energy; green, the healing of the mind and the body. A blue candle suggests emotional healing. If you like, you can concentrate on the flame of the candle while practicing your Bliss Breathing. A housekeeping note: It's important to place your candle in the center for safety reasons; you'll want to display items around it, but not so close that they can easily catch fire. Make sure, too, that the candle is far enough away from surrounding objects that might possibly catch fire, such as a curtain, paper, or a kitchen towel.

Many shops carry attractive glass votive candle holders. But keep in mind that you should not leave a candle unattended. Never go to work, for example, with a candle burning, thinking it will just go out on its own.

❧ *Flowers:*

Fresh-cut flowers bring lightness and freshness to your tranquility altar. In Asian society, it's believed that flowers are a tangible link to the forces of the spiritual world. Using them offers a gentle reminder from nature of your center of peace. The beauty of flowers alone can still the mind and provide a visual respite from your busy day. If you like, you can use artificial flowers on your tranquility altar. Even a picture of a flower, pretty bush, or colorful plant will do. Like candle colors, each type of flower has a unique symbolic signficance, and these vary culturally. Here are a few flowers I use and recommend for their significance and beauty:

Gardenias: A beautiful fragrant white flower that signifies joy and spiritual peace, gardenias are often used in ashrams and monasteries. They're typically seasonal, depending on where you live, and may have to be special-ordered from your local florist, but they're worth it. You can feel the transformative presence of a gardenia when you walk into a room; that's how powerfully fragrant they are.

Irises: Come in various colors such as blue, purple, and white. My dear florist friend tells me that the Telstar Iris from California lasts the longest—an average of 5 days.

White roses: Represent silence and purity.

Chrysanthemums: Signify optimism and cheerfulness.

Tulips: Come in various joyous colors and represent sweetness and light.

Hybrid Lily (Stargazer): Used in holy places of worship like churches, ashrams, and temples, these beautiful flowers do well alone or in small numbers. The best colors to use as a reminder of your Bliss Principle are yellow, white, and pink.

Orchid Plant (phaleonopsis): This plant of serenity is a great substitute for loose flower arrangements. They last for 2 to 4 months.

BLISS TIP:

It's best to place flowers in arrangements of odd numbers (1, 3, or 5) on your tranquility altar. According to some systems of numerology and feng shui, odd numbers represent a sense of balance.

❦ Crystals:

Vastu Shastra, a Hindu version of feng shui which considers all objects and spaces to be potential venues for healing, recommends using precious stones and crystals in tranquility altars because of their purifying effects. Crystals are nature's batteries. They energize and revitalize any personal space. Many churches, ashrams, and monasteries now place crystals in sacred spaces because of their spiritual power. As with candles and flowers, a crystal's color has symbolic meaning.

There is an endless array of precious stones you can use on your tranquility altar, but here are three basic crystals that I recommend:

Clear Quartz: This is among the most common and versatile of crystals. Clear quartz crystal is thought to have cleansing power and the ability to amplify and raise the vibrational energy of any space. Its color ranges from clear to opaque white.

Rose Quartz: Pink in color, this crystal is excellent for facilitating emotional clearing and healing. It's said to "tune" the one who holds it. The strength of the color pink cleanses, renews, and restores. Consider it a symbolic way to clear your head.

Amethyst: A brilliant purple stone, amethyst is thought to resonate and align one with the spiritual energy centers of the body known as the crown chakra, which is derived from the

Sanskrit word meaning "wheel." Amethyst is believed to help the mind become still and to calm stressful environments, especially in a work setting.

You can also use your birthstone in your tranquility altar, which may hold special significance for you. Thanks to the evolving study of crystal healing, many crystals and stones come with definitions and descriptions of their therapeutic uses. It's a good idea to do some research on different types.

OPTIONAL ALTAR ITEMS

In addition to a candle, flowers, and crystals, you might also want to add other items to your tranquility altar, or even add or delete them as you go along, changing them with your mood or the seasons. Consider your tranquility altar a work in progress, something that's fluid, like a stream. Here are some additional suggestions:

❧ *Photo or Image:*

A photo of a tranquil nature scene, such as the ocean or a sunset, can help capture the beauty and serenity a place has to offer and serve as a powerful reminder of nature and its healing properties. A picture of a saint, a peaceful animal, or even yourself as a child can also work. Just be sure to pick a photo or image that resonates with you, evoking pleasant, peaceful feelings or memories.

❧ A Quote or Prayer:

A spiritual prayer, mantra passage, or motivational saying can be an excellent focal point for your altar, because words have the power to transform, especially if you're a literary sort.

❧ A Bell:

The chiming of bells in ancient and modern-day Zen Buddhist monasteries and ashrams is a regular ritual that serves to subtly transform us through sound. Considered to be a spiritual act, bell ringing is intended to awaken the spiritual energies within us and within our surroundings. In Indian Hindu temples today, the spiritual act of performing *Arati*, a form of worship that waves a candle flame in front of one's chosen deity or teacher, is accompanied by the ringing of a bell to awaken the energy of grace. You can do the same by including a small bell in your tranquility altar to ring when you encounter your altar at the start of your day. A bell provides an audible reminder of your Bliss Principle within.

❧ A Water Fountain:

Having the sound of flowing water in your tranquility altar can soothe even the most restless soul. Like sitting beside a babbling book, a water fountain invites the wonderful serene influence that flowing water has on the emotions. (Water fountains specifically made for tranquility altars can easily be found online and on my Web site at www.takingcareofyou.com.)

❦ Burning Incense:

Through its pungent aroma, burning incense helps to create a peaceful mood and promotes a vibrational clearing in any space or environment. Popular incense scents for a tranquility altar that can lend an empowering peace include jasmine, juniper, myrrh, lavender, and the highly spiritual frankincense.

LOCATION, LOCATION, LOCATION

Once you construct your altar, you'll want to know where to put it. For many, indeed, the issue of available space and convenience may be a primary factor. For others, how private—or visible—it will be is a key consideration. Some of my clients like high-traffic areas such as the living room or the foyer of their house or apartment because they'll be sure to pass by and see it often. Others who prefer privacy opt for their bedroom or the area where they meditate. I have some clients who've constructed a tranquility altar tucked in a corner of their office. Even a dingy cubicle can become a healing haven.

If you would like a tranquility altar for your office as a reminder of your Bliss Principle while on the job, where some of us need it most, but you're uncomfortable displaying one for all your coworkers to see, do a modified version. Simply place some small amethyst crystals on or around your overworked computer (a personal favorite transformation tool of mine). Taking a quick look at a beautiful piece of purple amethyst can be like going to the beach for a few moments in between answering your busy phone and checking your e-mail. Posting photos of loved ones, of relaxing places, of a vacation you've been on, or of places you want to go can help provide a much-needed respite from the stress at hand. When you're at your desk, it's easy to get lost in whatever is going on. Looking at a pleasant picture temporarily takes you someplace else. Fresh-cut flowers can also help provide balance, as can a memento from your childhood.

I usually keep two tranquility altars, one in a special corner of my living room, which is my meditation area, and another in my kitchen, which gets the most attention. I often light my candle before I make my tea or breakfast and say a morning prayer. I typically stand before it and mentally offer up all the dramas that might be coming my way for that day. The kitchen is probably the most popular spot for a tranquility altar because, for most of us, it's the focal point and most well-used room in the house. Many of my clients like it because they can gaze at their altar as they start their day. Yes, it's a form of multitasking, but in a healthy way.

Tips for keeping your tranquility altar clean:

- *Try to change your flowers regularly.*
- *Dust and/ or wipe down your tranquility altar with rose water. Rose water keeps this space sweet and clean. Just purchase rose water from a local botanical or health food store. Add a few drops of rose water to a damp cloth or sponge and completely dust everything on your altar.*
- *Try to clean your crystal once a month to rid it of any dust and to give it a recharge.*

    Fill the kitchen sink with cold water, high enough to submerge the crystals. I add a little kosher salt or sea salt to the water, about 1 to 3 tablespoons depending how large or how many crystals there are, and allow them to soak for 5 to 10 minutes. I then rinse them with cold water and allow them to air dry on a thick towel.

CAPTURE THE POWER
OF SCENT

In addition to your tranquility altar, I also recommend aromatherapy, using the fragrant scent of essential oils made from flower essences, aromatic tree barks, and fruits to help elicit your Bliss Principle. Just a dab or two behind your ear or a whiff from time to time can instantly tame and calm the mind and emotions and soothe tense muscles.

You can also use aromatherapy in your bath. In fact, an aroma oil bath is a perfect way to combine the therapeutic benefits of aroma oils with the transformative medium of water. A thoroughly relaxing experience, an aroma oil bath eases body tightness and tension. Basic essential oils that help to create an inner and outer center of peace include:

❧ Peppermint/Spearmint:

These cooling and invigorating oils can help combat headaches and burnout.

❧ Ylang Ylang:

This oil fragrance is extremely effective for calming jittery nerves; the sense of relaxation it brings is instantaneous.

❧ Lavender:

This highly calming and relaxing fragrance is excellent for insomnia and anxiety.

❧ Sandalwood:

Aromatherapists value sandalwood oil because of its ability to soothe the mind and boost the immune system, as well as relieve stress and ease depression. Used in sacred ceremonies in the temples of the Far East for thousands of years, sandalwood is grown in India and Asia, the best grades are tapped from mature, forty- to sixty-year-old trees.

You can also diffuse essential oils in the air throughout a room to remind you of your innate peace by dabbing three to four drops of essential oil on a tissue, then placing that tissue in your personal space. Or try using steam to diffuse the aroma: Simply pour two cups of boiling water into a bowl and add up to ten drops of essential oil. (Use fewer drops if you are using strong oils that can irritate sensitive skin or nasal membranes, such as cinnamon, eucalyptus, pine, and lemon.) Steam heat helps the soothing aroma quickly pervade a room.

PILLOW POWER

So often the *peace urges* we have make it impossible to have a sound sleep. If you're having trouble falling asleep, try this natural aromatherapy pillow. Filled with actual flower essences (rather than essential oil), it promotes relaxation and restful sleep.

INGREDIENTS:

Cotton zippered pillowcase

⅓ pound rose petals

⅓ pound chamomile flowers

⅓ pound lavender petals

**(Flowers are available at health foods stores
and other places where aromatherapy is
sold)**

Declump and mix the aromatherapy flowers together; remove stems and prickly thorns. Pour mixture into a cotton pillowcase with zipper and shake them together until combined. Smooth out pillow so that ingredients are evenly distributed. Place aromatherapy pillow with mixture into a clean pillowcase, and place on top of your regular sleeping pillow. As you make your bed, cover pillows with a top blanket to allow the scent from your aromatherapy pillow to seep into your regular sleeping pillow during the day.

When you're ready for bed, remove the aromatherapy pillow from the top of your pillow, and rest in the aroma left behind. Breathe deeply as you try to fall asleep and relax. Sweet dreams.

SOLE SUPPORT

You may have been sitting at a desk all afternoon, but by the evening you feel as though you spent the entire day on your feet. It's not your imagination. Our feet carry the weight of our bodies and our stress—and can always use some extra pampering. There's nothing like a rosemary and peppermint foot soak to help you unwind after a long day and restore circulation to tired tootsies. Here's a quick recipe for an invigorating soak that will help put the zest back in your step and some peace in those toes.

This is what you do:

Gather herbs. Get a fresh bunch of rosemary and peppermint leaves from your local health food or general food store.

Brew the potion. Boil 6 to 7 cups of water, and add ½ cup each of peppermint and rosemary leaves. Turn off the heat, and allow the mixture to steep and cool for 10 to 15 minutes.

Prepare the bath. Strain, and add 3 to 4 cups of the strained mixture to a foot basin. Add enough cool water so that you're able to soak your feet comfortably. You can add a couple of drops of olive oil to the soak for extra moisturizing, if desired.

Feel the calm. Soak for 15 to 20 minutes and enjoy.

DO A WORLD FAST

Another lifestyle tool I recommend is a world fast, a variation on the silent retreat, which I try to participate in once a year at a select ashram.

On a silent retreat, there's no talking for seven, ten, or more days. That means no cell phones, no casual conversation, no words at all! I once went on a month-long silent retreat. I wore a button that said "I'm in Silence" and I didn't utter a sound for an entire month. It was difficult at first—even disorienting—but it was this retreat that allowed me to first experience my own inner peace. The extended silence was profoundly cleansing.

You don't have to go to such extremes in order to create a clearing and get in touch with your Bliss Principle. For this real-world, modified version of the silent retreat, I suggest simply trying for just a day not to watch TV, read the newspaper, listen to the radio, and, if you can, turn off your cell phone. While you're at it, ignore the latest sale going on at the local department store and pay no attention to all the advertisements screaming for your attention from every street corner billboard and magazine article. Simply purge your life of consumer and media mania.

With the advent of e-mail, cell phones, and voice mail as well as the usual standbys—television, the newspaper, and radio—we've grown accustomed to being on constant sensory overload. It's easy to get caught up in the constant drama. It can be extremely liberating to eliminate the external noise and stimulation, if only for a day every now and then.

After doing a world fast for 24 hours, many of my clients say they notice a shift in their energy and feel lighter as they go about their day. "There's less of a drain on my life force," one reported. "I can hear myself think again. I have so many more ideas." Skeptical? I urge you to try a world fast for a day and take note of how you feel. Trust me. It's like going on vacation without going anywhere.

CHAPTER 5

Lifestyle Recipes to Feed Your Bliss Principle

Behind the harsh appearance of the world, there is a benign power.

—MARTIN LUTHER KING JR.

We know instinctively that certain foods can instantly transform us, taking us from light-headed and edgy to calm and satisfied. These foods force us to slow down and be in the present moment—to simply relax. As another part of my Bliss Life Program I advocate certain comfort foods that are easy to make and filled with nourishment to support the immune system against the hazards of constant stress.

In Ayurveda, certain foods are identified as natural stress busters: walnuts, almonds, coconut, lightly cooked fruits such as pears, apples, and berries, milk, yogurt, fresh green leafy vegetables, and cheeses such as ricotta. If you are feeling particularly stressed, try to get more of these ingredients into your diet.

In addition, we can remind ourselves of our Bliss Principle while we nourish the body, mind, and spirit by paying attention to the way that we eat and drink, one breath at a time. Simply eat mindfully and with the awareness that your Bliss Principle waits behind each sip and spoonful you take. You can also take a Bliss Breath after you complete your meal.

BLISS LIFE PROGRAM MENU: HEALING TEA RECIPES

Known to heal mild anxiety, ease the common cold, and bring order to an upset stomach, herbal teas have long been regarded for their therapeutic properties. In recent years, herbal teas have been marketed for stress relief, and I believe in their bliss-inducing potential. I've discovered from personal experience that they relax the body and assist in creating a center of peace. Herbal teas also contain another essential ingredient: water! We all know how important it is to stay well-hydrated, and it is particularly true when we are under stress. Proper hydration helps boost the immune system, reduces fatigue, and assists the body in battling stress and anxiety. Just sitting down with a cup of herbal tea can still the mind and allow you to catch up with yourself. You can even use an herbal tea time-out as a prelude to practicing your Bliss Breathing.

Teas containing chamomile are especially known to bring health and balance to the body and mind. Valued for relieving nervousness and tension quickly, chamomile tea, in particular, is served routinely in hospitals throughout Europe to calm patients before surgery. Peppermint herbal tea is also an excellent elixir for stress. It can loosen tightness in the body and quell edginess.

Both herbs can be easily cultivated on your kitchen windowsill or outside garden, or purchased at your local health food store. They complement each other; while one (chamomile) is mild and naturally sweet, the other (peppermint) is spunky and cooling. As you'll see in the recipe that follows, I combine the two to give you the best of both worlds.

Chamomile and Peppermint Tea

Place 2 teaspoons of dried cut peppermint leaves and 2 teaspoons of dried chamomile flowers into a small plastic bag. Shut the bag tightly and shake until herbs are well combined. Remove the herb mix from the bag and place it into a teapot filled with 3 cups of boiling water. Allow the tea to steep for 10 minutes.

Strain the tea into a teacup and add a touch of honey, if desired. Take small, slow, and mindful sips. Breathe deeply and relax as you drink.

Ginger Tea

Ginger, a spice made from a root, also contains healing properties and is excellent eaten raw or served as tea. Ginger is thought to be good for circulation that may be impeded by stress. It is also a wonderful stimulant and inner lubricant for muscles and organs. Ginger is used throughout Asian culture as a multipurpose healing herb.

To make ginger tea:

Combine 1 cup of juiced ginger (available in health food stores, or make it yourself by pulverizing one large gingerroot in a food processor) with the juice of three lemons or limes. Add a touch of maple syrup or raw honey, if desired. To that, add one quart of purified water. Heat slightly or drink at room temperature. Be sure to take small, slow, and mindful sips and relax.

Soup is great comfort food. It warms and soothes and encourages you to focus on the present moment, spoonful by spoonful. And like herbal tea, it nourishes and relaxes the body all at the same time. Miso soup is one of my personal favorites. Its slightly salty broth is great for boosting the immune system. Balanced and earthy, miso soup is easy to make but you can also buy it ready-made in health food stores, Asian groceries, and, of course, in Japanese restaurants. Here, my rendition:

Miso Soup

INGREDIENTS:

2 ½ cups water

1 scallion, chopped (optional)

1 teaspoon minced fresh ginger

Optional Hearty Extras: Feel free to add 1 to 3 of the items below; more than that and the soup can become too crowded

½ cup thinly sliced mushrooms

½ cup peas

½ cup carrots

¼ cup firm tofu, cut into ¾" cubes

1 stick wakame sea vegetables (available in Asian markets)

½ cup assorted mixed vegetables

1 tablespoon miso paste dissolved in one
   tablespoon water

½ teaspoon sesame oil

1 to 2 teaspoons Tamari/soy sauce to taste

In a medium saucepan combine the water, scallions (if using), and ginger. Bring to a boil over high heat. Add hearty extras mentioned above, as desired. Reduce heat to low, and simmer for 3 to 5 minutes until all ingredients are slightly softened. Remove from heat and stir in dissolved miso and sesame oil, then add tofu. Let soup sit for about 2 minutes. Pour soup through a strainer into serving bowls; add back a few of the strained items as garnish, if desired. Serves 4.

Creamy Pea Soup

This is a great soup to make on a rainy Sunday or when you have a little extra time. Hearty and filling, it is particularly satisfying when eaten one breath at a time.

INGREDIENTS:

1 tablespoon olive oil

2 ½ cups fresh or frozen peas or chopped sugar
   snap peas

1 potato, peeled and cubed

1 small head of Bibb or Boston lettuce,
   chopped

6 cups water or vegetable stock

Salt and pepper to taste

Shredded fresh mint, cilantro, or basil leaves,
   for garnish

Place 1 tablespoon of oil, peas, potato, and lettuce in a large pot and sauté (don't fry) over medium-low heat for 5 minutes. Add the water or stock and bring to a boil. Lower the heat, cover, and simmer until vegetables are very tender, about 20 minutes.

In a food processor or blender, puree the soup until creamy. Return to pot and reheat slowly. Season with salt and pepper. Serve in shallow bowls and garnish with the herbs. Serves 6.

Lite Broccoli-Cheese Soup

INGREDIENTS:

6 fresh broccoli spears

Nonstick vegetable spray or olive oil

¼ cup finely chopped onions

½ cup water

10-ounce can 98-percent fat-free broccoli-
cheese soup

¾ cup nonfat or low fat milk

Optional Garnishes: Parsley, fresh chopped
tomatoes, spears of cooked broccoli,
chopped bell peppers

Chop 5 broccoli spears, leaving one whole. Heat non-stick saucepan over medium heat; coat with nonstick spray. Add onion, sautéing about 2 minutes. Add water and bring to a simmer, then add broccoli, including the whole spear. Cook until tender, about 5 minutes. Remove whole broccoli spear. Stir in soup and milk until mixed. Simmer 5 minutes. To serve, sprinkle with one or more garnishes if desired and top each bowl with half a broccoli spear. Serves 2.

SUPPORTIVE SALADS, SMOOTHIES, AND STEWS

The salad, smoothie, and stew recipes that follow provide a cornucopia of fruits and vegetables that are loaded with anti-oxidants (nutrients that help neutralize free radicals, the unstable oxygen molecules produced by the body that can damage cell DNA). Antioxidants help support the immune system and counter the ill effects of chronic stress.

Green Oriental Salad

INGREDIENTS:

1 cup torn lettuce, such as romaine, Boston, or
    mesclun

1 cup torn Chinese Napa cabbage

1 cup mung bean sprouts

½ cup trimmed snow peas

½ cup canned sliced bamboo shoots, rinsed

¼ cup thinly sliced celery

¼ cup chopped broccoli

DRESSING:

3 tablespoons low-sodium soy sauce

3 tablespoons rice vinegar

2 tablespoons water

¼ teaspoon minced garlic

¼ teaspoon minced fresh gingerroot

Combine all salad ingredients in a large bowl. Toss to
mix. Set aside. Combine all the dressing ingredients in a
blender, food processor, or lidded jar. Process briefly or
shake well to combine. Pour over salad and toss to coat.
Serves 4.

Peaceful Squash Stew

INGREDIENTS:

1 onion, diced

3 cloves garlic, minced

2 tablespoons oil of choice

3 cups pumpkin or butternut squash, peeled, seeded, and chopped

2 potatoes, peeled and chopped

2 tablespoons whole-wheat flour

2 cups vegetable stock or water

¾ tablespoon ground cinnamon

2 tablespoons apple cider vinegar

1 cup frozen peas

1 cup frozen whole-kernel corn

Salt and pepper to taste

Cook the onion and garlic in oil of choice, stirring until the onion is transparent, about 4 minutes. Add the squash and potatoes. Cook, while stirring occasionally, for 5 minutes. Stir in the flour until dissolved. Add the vegetable stock or water, cinnamon, and vinegar, and simmer over medium-low heat, stirring occasionally until the sauce is thick and the vegetables are tender, about 30 minutes. Add the peas and corn and cook 5 minutes more. Season with salt and pepper. Serves 4.

BLISS TIP:

If possible, try to serve your comfort food in a deep ceramic bowl or cup. The dishes that you use to eat and drink can also help you remember your Bliss Principle. A solid ceramic bowl has a satisfying weight and texture, and will absorb warmth from the beverage or food contained within.

Indian Vegetable Stew

INGREDIENTS:

½ tablespoon butter or margarine

1 tablespoon safflower oil

2 garlic cloves, minced

1 ½ tablespoons minced fresh gingerroot

1 teaspoon ground cumin

½ teaspoon ground coriander

¼ teaspoon ground cloves

½ teaspoon ground cardamom

¼ teaspoon dry mustard

½ teaspoon ground turmeric

½ stick cinnamon

1 teaspoon salt

3 cups vegetable stock

3 teaspoons fresh lime juice

1 tablespoon honey

3 carrots, sliced diagonally

1 ½ cups thickly sliced button mushrooms

2 cauliflower florets

1 medium russet potato, diced

In a large saucepan, melt the butter or margarine over medium heat and add the oil. Cook the garlic and ginger, stirring for 1 minute. Add the cumin, coriander, cloves, cardamom, mustard, turmeric, cinnamon, and salt. Stir and cook 2 minutes to release the flavors. Add the stock, lime juice, and honey, and cook 3 to 4 minutes more. Add the vegetables, cover, and cook until tender, about 25 minutes. Discard the cinnamon stick. Serves 4.

SMOOTHIES

Very Berry Smoothies

INGREDIENTS:

1 cup fresh blueberries

1 cup blueberry yogurt

½ cup apple juice, or soy or almond milk

4 ice cubes

2 tablespoons protein powder

Combine all ingredients in a blender or food processor and process until smooth. Serves 1.

PACIFYING PASTA

Smooth yet slightly chewy, pasta is the ultimate comfort food. Here's a favorite pasta recipe of mine that helps take the edge off a hectic day and otherwise warms us from the inside out. Chock-full of life-giving vegetables, the dish has healing properties all its own.

Penne with Balsamic-Roasted Vegetables

INGREDIENTS:

2 small eggplants (about ½ pound each), quartered lengthwise and cut into 1-inch cubes

2 ripe beefsteak tomatoes cut into 1-inch pieces

16 baby carrots

⅓ cup plus 1 tablespoon balsamic vinegar, divided

2 tablespoons chopped fresh oregano, or 2 teaspoons dried

2 tablespoons olive oil

½ teaspoon salt

½ teaspoon freshly ground black pepper

12 ounces uncooked penne pasta

1 cup reduced-sodium, nonfat chicken or
vegetable broth

½ cup vermouth or dry white wine

4 tablespoons grated parmigiano-reggiano or
other Parmesan cheese (you can use soy
cheese too)

Nonstick cooking spray

Preheat oven to 450° F. In a large bowl, combine eggplant, tomatoes, carrots, ⅓ cup of the balsamic vinegar, oregano, 1 tablespoon of the olive oil, and salt and pepper. Toss to coat. Arrange vegetables on a large baking sheet that has been lightly coated with cooking spray, and roast 20 minutes or until golden brown and tender. Remove vegetables from oven and set aside. Cook penne in a large pot of rapidly boiling water until just tender, about 10 minutes. Drain and transfer to a large bowl. Add remaining tablespoons balsamic vinegar and olive oil, broth, and vermouth or white wine. Toss to coat. Add roasted vegetables; toss to combine. Spoon pasta and vegetables into deep bowls and top with grated Parmesan. Serves 4.

> ## Bliss Tip:
>
> To get more emotional fulfillment from your comfort meals and snacks, try creating an island of sacred space by eliminating distractions such as the TV and the phone. I also suggest lighting a candle for reflective ambience if the setting and timing call for it. Don't forget to do one round of Bliss Breathing before and after eating.

TRY MEALTIME MEDITATION

In addition to what you eat, pay attention to how *fast* you consume; it's just as important for nourishing your well-being. In this era of dashboard dining and cubicle cuisine, our meals are literally becoming a feeding frenzy. You may want to try eating mindfully like the Buddhist monks do: Eat slowly and examine your food as if you were looking at it for the first time. Really pay attention. Then concentrate on slowing down. Make your movements twice as deliberate and fluid as they normally are as you bring each fork or spoonful to your mouth. Savor the flavors and textures. Finally, don't think about the next thing you have to do. Just be.

CHAPTER 6

Personalizing Your Bliss Life Program

Nothing really matters but the Peace inside your soul.

— KELLYE DAVIS

As you practice the Bliss Life Program, from your Bliss Breathing, meditation, and the Relaxation Workout, to the Bliss Maintenance tools for transformation, you may find yourself wondering how you can personally apply it all. The whole notion of recognizing and accessing your Bliss Principle might be foreign initially, and trying to fit the pieces of the program into your life might feel overwhelming. So how can you pull it all together or select the most important elements to quench your unique *peace urge?*

The secret is to personalize the Bliss Life Program according to the type of *peace urge* you are experiencing. Personalizing your Bliss Life Program goes hand in hand with your *peace urge* profile, which you learned about by taking the *Peace Urge* Quiz in the Introduction to this book. Like having brown eyes and curly hair or looking better in blue than chartreuse, your *peace urge* profile is unique to you. In addition, your profile will change according to the specific demands being made on you. This week you might be on hyperdrive and unable to slow down and relax, but next week feel short-tempered and as tired as a worn-out rag. By personalizing your program so that it dovetails with your unique *peace urge* type, you will find accessing your bliss principle that much easier whenever you feel the need.

In the following sections, I have outlined custom Bliss Life Program prescriptions which target the most common *peace urge* profiles. You may find that you fall somewhere in between, so feel free to mix and match the ingredients as they apply to you.

> # PEACE URGE PROFILE
>
> I feel numb or depressed much of the time.

BLISSRX:

Often when we live with an excess of stress over a period of time, we can literally become weighed down and caught in a mental fog. We can't think, move freely, or process our feelings. We feel depressed and numb and are stuck in stressful energy from which we can't break free. It's like being caught in a web where we are chained to stressful energy. In order to relieve this *peace urge*, we need to create a psychological and spiritual clearing.

Here's a personalized daily program you can implement when you choose:

Practice daily conscious deep breathing, or three-part breathing, at strategic times throughout the day.

Refresher: Simply focus on your breath as you inhale and exhale through your nose. Follow the breath as your abdomen rises and falls with each complete inhalation and exhalation. Now close your eyes and take two to ten deep breaths while paying attention to each breath. As you inhale, allow the breath to rise all the way from your belly button to your heart, and all the way up to your collarbone. Continue to follow your breath in this fashion as it comes in and goes out. You might even want to place your hand on your abdomen and feel it rise and fall in sync with each breath. A couple of conscious breaths work wonders and can brush away minor traces of depression and help to invigorate your awareness, while tuning you in to your Bliss Principle vibration.

Do a periodic world fast. The purpose of the world fast is to cleanse yourself of information overload. For just one day every now and then, tune out the outside world. Don't watch TV, don't read the newspaper, and keep the radio turned off. If you're in your car, keep the dial tuned to relaxation music. Make it a meditative journey by noticing the scenery as it passes by, or focus on your breath.

Don't check your e-mail or answer your cell phone for the day. Although you may find a world fast disorienting at first, I think you'll find it healing as you grow accustomed to the quiet and respite it provides.

Try to do the complete version of the Relaxation Workout at least two times a week or whenever you can.

Spend time on Bliss Move 1: Corpse Pose with Deep Conscious Breathing. If you don't have time to do the entire Bliss Relaxation Workout, try to at least fit this move in when you need a quick stress fix. This move can help silence all the busy thoughts and relaxes the body so you are ready to feel the healing benefits of the Bliss Principle.

Refresher: To start, lie on your back with your eyes closed and your arms resting comfortably at your sides with your palms facing up. Allow your feet to naturally turn out and let the weight of your head, shoulders, back, pelvis, and legs melt down into the floor. Bring awareness to your breath; follow your breath as you inhale and exhale, and continuously breathe deeply. Do this for about 1 minute.

For general bliss maintenance, be sure to create a tranquility altar, or better yet, two: perhaps one at work and one at home. Place them in visible spots, even if they are only visible to you. Start with a tray or mat and take care to hand-select symbolic objects that you associate with peace: the right scented candle, flowers, and crystals, a tranquil photo or image, a quote or prayer, a bell, a water fountain, or burning incense.

A special note: Keep your tranquility altar fresh with white flowers and with a white candle. Put several pieces of quartz crystals on it to amplify the positive energy. Say a prayer or burn incense and use your tranquility altar on a daily basis to remember the Bliss Principle within.

> # PEACE URGE PROFILE
>
> I'm always on the go and can't relax, even though I know I'm exhausted.

BLISSRX:

If this is your *peace urge*, you are pushing against the river of life and cannot slow down to catch the wave of the present moment. You have trouble allowing yourself the necessary periods of rest that can open a path to your Bliss Principle. Creating a clearing, physically and psychologically, is the key to relieving this type of *peace urge*.

Here's a personalized daily program you can implement when you choose:

Remember to start the day off peacefully. Surrendering to peaceful morning rituals that create a relaxed mood before the day even begins help to set the tone for the entire day.

Morning ritual tips:
- *Take an aroma shower. Spurt a couple of drops of lemon or ylang ylang essential oil into the flowing shower and inhale the aroma as you do a couple of deep breaths.*

⊖ *Burn soothing incense that has lavender, sandalwood, or frankincense in the morning on your tranquility altar.*

⊖ *Play instrumental, chanting, or spiritual music as you get dressed, sip on some herbal tea, and prepare for the day.*

Try to practice your Bliss Breathing daily at strategic times throughout the day, especially when you feel over-extended and rushed.

Step 1: Sit upright and relaxed. Become aware of the present moment by consciously focusing on your breathing. The key word here is consciously. Remember to experience your breathing. Just notice it.

Step 2: Begin taking deep, conscious breaths in and out through your nose. Imagine filling yourself with life-giving oxygen from your belly button all the way to the top of your collarbones. Then exhale "long," as I like to say, through your nose. As you inhale and exhale through your nose, stay focused on the sound and feel of each breath. You're creating the clearing to connect with your Bliss Principle.

Step 3: Close your eyes, if you can (you may not be able to do so if you're in public), and as you continue to focus on your breathing, feel the stillness and silence in your body. Continue to follow your breath with awareness for 30 seconds.

Step 4: Take a retention breath. With your eyes still closed, inhale and hold the breath for 2 seconds, then slowly exhale through your mouth with slightly parted lips. Feel your muscles relax as you complete the exhale. Then continue taking deep, oxygenated, conscious breaths for 30 seconds.

Step 5: Take another retention breath by inhaling and holding the breath for 2 seconds, then slowly exhaling through your mouth. Then continue taking deep, oxygenated, conscious breaths for 30 seconds. Deep, conscious breathing is your default mode.

Step 6: Take your final retention breath by inhaling and holding the breath for 2 seconds, then slowly exhaling through your mouth. Then continue taking deep, oxygenated, conscious breaths for 30 seconds.

Step 7: Finally, open your eyes and breathe naturally without too much focus. Gently gaze at any still object before you that catches your eye, such as your hands, legs, or feet, a tree, the ground, or a wall, and feel the stillness and silence in that body part or object.

Try to do the complete version of the Relaxation Workout at least two times a week or whenever you can.

Spend time doing Bliss Move 9. If meditation works for you, spend more time on Bliss Move 9 while doing the Relaxation Workout. This move helps to create a clearing in the mind from stressful thoughts while encouraging you to slow down and fall into the natural rhythm of life.

Refresher: Bring yourself up into a cross-legged position. Gently close your eyes and relax into the still darkness before you. Follow your breath with each inhalation and exhalation, one breath at a time. If thoughts come up, ignore them and keep your awareness on your breath. Try to sit a little longer than usual by 5 minutes or more. If you have more time, feel free to sit longer. You can also apply the essential oil of sandalwood or an oil of choice to your meditation by putting a couple of drops in a tissue and taking a few whiffs before you sit to meditate.

BLISS TIP: TAKE YOUR SHOES OFF

When you get home at the end of the day, immediately remove your shoes as you enter the house to ground yourself in your home environment. If you think you'll be home for the rest of the evening, leisurely apply some lavender oil to your feet before you prepare dinner or begin your evening activities. This will help you relax into the present moment and remind you that the rush you experienced all day has come to an end.

PEACE URGE PROFILE

I am freqently short-tempered and angry and
feel the weight of the world on my shoulders.

BlissRx:

Frequent, unexpected flare-ups of anger and a short temper
can be a signal that you are ignoring your stress. Creating an
emotional clearing is the key to relieving this type of *peace
urge*.

*Here's a personalized daily program you can implement as you
choose:*

Walking Meditation: A meditative walk is a great way to
connect with nature's peace and silence. Take a walk into
your local park or garden. Choose a tree, bush, or flower that
appeals to you. Look at it closely and bring your awareness to
your breath. Observe the stillness and silence of the plant.
Now feel the peace of this simple organism and take that
peace into your being.

Practice Bliss Breathing and the Relaxation Workout
at least once a day. **Spend time on Bliss Move 2: Yoga
Nidra.** Allow extra time to focus on the Yoga Nidra move.

You'll systematically tense and release each part of your body to yield a deep sense of calm. Bliss Move 2 is especially useful when the Relaxation Workout or a walking meditation is not an option.

Refresher: Get in the Corpse Pose, and go directly from head to toe tensing and releasing the muscles in each body part as directed below.

Step 1: Bring awareness to the face. Gently move your jaw up and down and side to side. Relax. Close your eyes and relax them. With your eyes closed, raise your eyebrows. Then wrinkle your forehead. Relax. Take a deep conscious breath. Gently open your eyes and resume normal breathing.

Step 2: Gently roll your head from side to side, mentally relaxing your neck muscles. Return your head to center and relax. Take a deep conscious breath and resume normal breathing.

Step 3: Leaving your arms on the floor, lift your shoulders and squeeze them together in front of your chest. Squeeze and relax. Then bring your shoulders up toward your ears. Squeeze and relax. Take a deep conscious breath and resume normal breathing.

Step 4: To bring awareness to both of your arms, make a fist of both hands. Then tighten your arms and raise them up slightly off the floor. Release and roll your arms gently from side to side and let them melt into the floor. Take a deep conscious breath and resume normal breathing.

Step 5: Exhale and inhale deeply through your nose,

puffing up your abdomen like a balloon, taking in as much air as you can, and then a little bit more. Hold the breath for 7 seconds, then release and relax your abdomen. Take a deep conscious breath and resume normal breathing.

Step 6: To bring awareness to the buttocks, squeeze the buttock muscles tight; try to raise them slightly off the floor. Relax. Take a deep conscious breath and resume normal breathing.

Step 7: Bring awareness to both legs: squeeze and tighten the muscles, starting in your calves and moving up to your thighs. Release. Take a deep conscious breath and resume normal breathing.

Be sure to create a tranquility altar. If it's not possible to create a full altar at work, simply put a single white flower, such as a gardenia, white rose, or lily, in a bowl on or near your desk or computer. The power of one flower is a great meditative focal point that can center your emotions when you feel the anger rising. Take deep, conscious breaths as you let the flower remind you that there is a supreme peace behind all stressful situations.

PEACE URGE PROFILE

I'm often anxious and tend to worry excessively over small problems.

BlissRx:

Excessive worry over small, expectable problems creates an enormous drain, both psychologically and emotionally. It is almost impossible to access your Bliss Principle if you are in a constant battle with anxiety. Creating a psychological clearing where you are free of the disturbing mental chatter that accompanies chronic anxiety is key to relieving this type of *peace urge*.

Here's a personalized daily program that you can implement when you choose:

Use the power of a mantra. Choose a short positive or spiritual concentration phrase to repeat to yourself as stress and anxiety begins to build. "Be calm" or "cool, relaxed mind, calm body" can work wonders to stem the tide of worry that threatens to engulf you. Or, if spiritual phrases feel comfortable to you, try, "The Lord is my shepherd," or "Oh, great spirit," or simply, "Om." Again, choose a mantra that resonates with you and will bring calm and focus when you need it most.

Use lavender in many ways. Keep and burn a lavender candle on your tranquility altar for a few weeks at a time. Also, meditate with lavender essential oil by applying a dab on each pulse point with a cotton swab before you sit to meditate. Lavender is a flower essence widely used by herbalists and aromatherapists and is one of the few calming scents that can be applied undiluted. Its calming aroma can be used to treat various *peace urge* challenges caused by constant stress and anxiety.

Practice Bliss Breathing and the Relaxation Workout at least once a day. **Spend a little extra time on Bliss Move 6: Crocodile Pose.** This Bliss Move soothes the nervous system that is bombarded by anxiety and excessive worry.

Refresher: Lie on your stomach with your arms folded at head level. Rest your forehead comfortably on folded arms. Observe the rising and falling of your abdomen as it expands and contracts with each breath. Feel yourself become more and more relaxed with each breath you take as you connect with the stillness of the floor. Do this for 3 to 5 minutes.

Aroma Pillow Deep Sleep. If you are plagued by anxious thoughts, you may find falling asleep at night difficult. Keeping a lavender, chamomile, and rose aroma pillow sachet on top of your nighttime pillow during the day will let you enjoy its relaxing aroma at bedtime. See instructions on how to make an aroma pillow in Chapter 4.

Be sure to prepare a cup of herbal tea once a day or whenever you can, preferably the chamomile and peppermint recipe. See Chapter 5 for tea recipes.

PEACE URGE PROFILE

I suffer from frequent colds, headaches, or
minor stomach ailments.

BLISSRX:

The body never lies. It speaks to us through frequent colds,
headaches, stomach problems, or other minor ailments. Always consult your physician first if you feel unwell, but if
you and your physician have ruled out a diagnosable medical
condition, your body may simply be telling you that you need
to restore and replenish your system. Creating a clearing
physically is the key to relieving this type of *peace urge*.

*Here's a personalized daily program you can implement when
you choose:*

Do the Relaxation Workout as often as you can.
Spend time on Bliss Move 5: Cat Cow Stretch. This
Bliss Move is great for clearing energy in the spine that gets
blocked when there is tension in the body.

Refresher: Come onto your hands and knees, aligning
your knees directly under your hips, palms to the floor with
fingers facing forward. As you inhale, drop your belly toward

the floor and raise your head back slightly toward your buttocks. Gently push through your hands and knees and feel an invigorating stretch in the front of your body and spine. As you exhale, go in the opposite direction. Point your toes and round your back and entire spine, tucking in your tailbone. Draw your chin to your chest. (Be sure to pull in abdomen while exhaling.) Feel the gentle stretch in the spine. Repeat the Cat Cow Stretch four times and then rest on your back in the Corpse Pose and do one complete Bliss Breath. Then relax for a few moments.

Use amethyst quartz crystals on and around you. Amethyst crystal is a versatile healing stone and can be very helpful in soothing physical signs of stress such as headaches, body stiffness, muscle twitches, and constant yawning. Crystals and gemstones like amethyst give off different types of frequencies that can help bring the body back into balance during periods of stress. You can carry a few small pieces on you—in your purse, briefcase, or pocket. Remember that when choosing any crystal or gemstone to support your Bliss Life Program, hold and feel the stone for a little while. Take a minute to explore it and make sure it feels right for you before you select it as your own.

Soothe a stress headache

Gather four small amethyst crystals—they should be small enough to be placed on the body without falling off. Lie on your back in the Corpse Pose. First, place one crystal above the crown of your head on the floor. Place the next crystal on your forehead at the space between the eyebrows. Place the remaining two pieces on the base of the neck allowing them to rest on the collarbone. Now close your eyes and take deep conscious breaths for at least 10 minutes and allow the energy of the stones to soak up and balance out all tension in the head and neck area. Relax.

Do a once-a-week foot soak while doing deep breathing. Foot soaks are therapeutic for the body and relieve stress. Try the Bliss Maintenance foot-soak recipe tip in Chapter 4 for soothing tired feet.

Drink a deep cup of ginger tea during lunchtime for its soothing and warming effects on the body. Try a bowl of miso soup a few times a week. Miso is especially known for its beneficial effects on the immune system. See recipes in Chapter 5.

Mindfulness in Action: Here's a great mindfulness technique to do while sipping tea, giving yourself a foot soak, or having a bowl of miso soup.

Smile: Bring a half-smile to your face and imagine one in your heart.

Breathe: Be aware of the wave of the breath as the breath comes in and goes out.

Focus: Concentrate only on what's in front of you or on

what you are doing right now. Examine the activity as if you're looking at it for the first time. Really pay attention.

Slow down: Make your movements twice as slow and fluid as you would normally. As you take a sip of tea, for example, feel the cup on your lip and feel the warmth as you swallow. During your foot soak, wave your feet slowly back and forth in the water and watch the ripples.

Just be for a little while.

PEACE URGE PROFILE

I find myself dreaming about having time just for me, but never manage to find it.

BLISSRx:

We all need time to ourselves. We all need to release, relax, and restore. But some of us never quite manage to give that time to ourselves. If you increasingly find yourself fantasizing about solitude, whether it's a vacation by yourself or just an afternoon of peace and quiet, that's your *peace urge*. Take that vacation you've been putting off. But if your finances or responsibilities won't even allow you an afternoon away from your routine, at least you can work on creating an environmental clearing that is key to relieving this type of *peace urge*.

Here's a personalized daily program you can implement when you choose:

Escape the stressful daily grind and monotony by doing your Bliss Breathing and Relaxation Workout as much as you can. Spend additional time in Bliss Move 8: Body Scan. In addition to its other therapeutic benefits, this move can allow you an excellent escape from the daily grind. Remember not to fall asleep: It's that re-laxing.

Refresher: As you do this Bliss Move, you'll lead your-self through a guided tour of your body. As you inhale, direct your breath to each targeted body part. As you exhale, relax that area of the body. Gently come onto your back and relax your spine down into the floor with arms alongside your body and your legs and feet relaxed.

Arms: As you inhale, imagine your arms filling with breath, then exhale slowly and relax your arms.

Shoulders: As you inhale, imagine your shoulders fill-ing with breath, then exhale slowly and relax your shoulders.

Neck: As you inhale, imagine your neck filling with breath, then exhale slowly and relax your neck.

Stomach: As you inhale, imagine your stomach filling with breath, then exhale slowly and relax your stomach.

Chest: As you inhale, imagine your chest filling with breath, then exhale slowly and relax your chest.

Face: As you inhale, imagine your face filling with breath, then exhale slowly and relax your face.

Top of Your Head: As you inhale, imagine the top of your head filling with breath, then exhale slowly and relax the top of your head. Finally, bring your awareness back to normal breathing and relax.

Do a world fast at least once a month on a weekend day and use your fast as an opportunity to reconnect

with nature. I recommend getting into the habit of going for a leisurely walk in the park, sitting by a river or the ocean, or watching the sunset. Try simply watching the birds around a bird feeder. Try to stay as silent and still as possible throughout the day as you engage in your world fast, free from everyday distractions like the TV, radio, and newspapers.

Create several tranquility altars in your home. At home you can place a tranquility altar in your kitchen, bedroom, and living room. Make each of them different in color and in your choice of flower, candle, and scents. For example, one can be white, denoting clarity, while another might be blue, signifying emotional harmony. Go to Chapter 4, Lifestyle Tools, and select some items that call out to you.

If it feels comfortable, try attending a religious service or joining a spiritual circle. Performing a sacred act can be a time to reconnect with yourself and may feel like a special gift to yourself.

Try visiting a day spa. It's a larger commitment of both time and money, but treating yourself to an afternoon or even an hour at a luxurious spa can work wonders. Choose a spa with an especially tranquil environment, such as candles and water fountains, where you can lose yourself in the peaceful atmosphere.

Select from the tea and soup recipes in Chapter 5. A tea-time break in the afternoon or a soothing bowl of soup at dinner can provide an interlude of quiet and solitude in your day.

RELAX, IT'S YOUR LIFE. . . . GOOD LUCK ON YOUR JOURNEY

As you practice and personalize your Bliss Life Program, you'll find that engaging your Bliss Principle—the natural peace inside your mind, body, and spirit—gets easier. Learning to engage your Bliss Principle, through the breathing, meditation, relaxation workout, and support tools for transformation I've suggested throughout this book, will soon become second nature to you. "I actually feel like I'm starting to rewire my life," one client told me, after putting her version of the Bliss Life Program into practice for several months.

I wish you similar success. No matter who you are or where you live, managing stress can be a big problem at certain times in your life. But you don't have to quit your job or take an expensive vacation to find relief and restoration. Take action with the Bliss Life Program, every day, throughout your day, one conscious breath at a time.

So, now it's up to you. Your Bliss Life is waiting!

Resources

General reading

- *Power Yoga,* by Beryl Bender Birch
- *Yoga: The Path to Holistic Health,* by B. K. S. Iyengar
- *The Seven Spiritual Laws of Yoga: A Practical Guide to Healing Body, Mind, and Spirit,* by Deepak Chopra and David Simon
- *Chant: Discovering Spirit in Sound,* by Robert Gass
- *Mystery of the Mind,* by Swami Muktananda
- *Quantum Healing,* by Deepak Chopra, M.D.

❧ Cookbooks for Gentle Meals

- *The Yoga Cookbook: Vegetarian Food for Body and Mind,* by The Sivananda Yoga Center
- *The Expanding Light Cookbook: Vegetarian Favorites from California's Premier Yoga Retreat,* by Blanche Agassy McCord
- *The Ayurvedic Cookbook,* by Amadea Morningstar and Urmila Desai

❧ Altars

- *Altars: Bringing Sacred Shrines into Your Everyday Life,* by Denise Linn
- *Creating Sacred Space With Feng Shui,* by Karen Kingston

❧ Aromatherapy

- *Aromatherapy Solutions,* by Veronica Sibley
- *Restore Yourself with Essential Oils,* by M. Lou Luchsinger

❧ Crystals

- *Crystals and Crystal Healing* (The New Life Library), by Simon Lilly

- *The Crystal Bible: A Definitive Guide to Crystals,* by Judy Hall

Magazines

- *Shambala Sun Magazine Resource* (www.shambalasun.com)
- *Body & Soul*
- *Yoga International*
- *Yoga Journal*
- *Real Simple*

USEFUL ADDRESSES

Places for Tea

Teany
90 Rivington St., NYC
212 475-9190

A Cuppa Tea
3202 College Ave.
Berkeley, CA 94705

Argo Tea Café
958 W. Armitage Ave.
Chicago, IL 60614
(312) 873-4123
www.argotea.com

The Four Seasons Hotel at Mandalay Bay Hotel [Tea room]
3960 Las Vegas Boulevard
South; Las Vegas, NV 89119
702-632-5000

The Urban Tea Lounge
838 W. Montrose Ave.
Chicago, IL 60613
(773) 907-URBN

Teafusions Teahouse
202 City Circle, Suite 120
Peachtree City, GA
770-486-5339

Babo Teahouse
10 River Drive South
Jersey City, NJ 07310
(201) 626-6006

Lady Effie's Tea Parlor
453 East Adams Blvd.
Los Angeles, CA 90011
(213) 749-2204
www.ladyeffiesteaparlor.com

WEB SITES

www.takingcareofyou.com
www.beliefnet.com
www.enlightenment.com
www.yoga.com
www.meditationcenter.com

SPAS TO NURTURE
THE BLISS PRINCIPLE

⊖ **The Chopra Center at La Costa Resort and Spa,**
2013 Costa del Mar Rd., Carlsbad, CA 92009

- **NewAge Health Spa,** PO Box 658, Rte. 55, Neversink, NY 12765
- **Body Essentials Day Spa and Ayurvedic Center,** 11 W. 36th St. 4th Fl., New York, NY 10018
- **Pura Vida USA Spa and Yoga Retreat,** 400 Blueberry Hill, Dahlonega, GA 30533

INTERNATIONAL SPAS

- **Aventura Spa Palace,** Km. 72, Carretera Cancun-Tulum, Riviera Maya, Q. Roo 77710 Mexico, www.palaceresorts.com
- **Ancient Cedars Spa,** Osprey Lane at Chesterman Beach, Box 250, Tofino, BC V0R 2Z0, Canada, www.wickinn.com
- **Hotel Byblos Andaluz & La Prairie Beauty Centre,** Mijas Golf, 29650 Mijas Costa, Malaga, Spain, www.byblos-andaluz.com
- **The Body Holiday at LeSPORT**, PO Box 437, Castries, St. Lucia, West Indies, www.thebodyholiday.com

⊖ Meditation Music (downloadable software at
www.homepage.mac.com), David Ahmed

⊖ Indian Meditation Music (downloadable software at
www.sanatansociety.org)

⊖ Guided Meditation, *Bodhipaksa* (www.wildmind.org)

⊖ Reiki Meditations (www.half.com)

⊖ Yoga Meditations (www.half.com)

⊖ Chakra Meditations (www.half.com), Ben Scott

⊖ Spa Song (www.spasong.com), various artists